The Effective Teacher's Guide to Behavioural, Emotional and Social Difficulties

Teaching and supporting pupils with behavioural, emotional and social difficulties is arguably the most challenging aspect of being a teacher today.

The Effective Teacher's Guide to Behavioural, Emotional and Social Difficulties provides busy teachers with an easily digestible yet thorough overview of the basic theories surrounding behaviour. The book also looks at the range of strategies that can be used in the classroom, and how their effectiveness can best be assessed. The range of different strategies presented and explained includes:

◆ cognitive approach
◆ systems-based approach
◆ behavioural approach
◆ psychodynamic approach.

Also included is a chapter devoted to supporting pupils with attention deficit hyperactivity disorder. The chapter contains information about identifying and assessing the condition and suggests effective intervention strategies, such as developing self-esteem and interpersonal skills.

Highly accessible and authoritative, and taking into account the very latest developments in the field of special educational needs, this book will prove invaluable reading for all busy practitioners eager to develop their knowledge and understanding.

Michael Farrell is an independent educational consultant and recognised expert in special education. He has written or edited over 30 acclaimed education books.

New Directions in Special Educational Needs

By focusing firmly on what really works in practice with children with special educational needs, this highly practical series will enlighten and inform any busy teacher eager to know more about individual difficulties, and who wants to make inclusion a reality for their pupils.

All books in the series concentrate on the educational implications of certain special educational needs. They also consider the legal obligations of schools, what teachers can do to support and encourage inclusive learning in their class-room, and where they can go for additional support and advice. Packed full of down-to-earth yet authoritative advice, this series will provide teachers with every-thing they need to ensure their pupils with special educational needs are effectively and properly supported.

Titles in the Series (all by Michael Farrell)

The Effective Teacher's Guide to Behavioural, Emotional and Social Difficulties
Practical strategies

The Effective Teacher's Guide to Autism and Communication Difficulties
Practical strategies

The Effective Teacher's Guide to Dyslexia and Other Specific Learning Difficulties
Practical strategies

The Effective Teacher's Guide to Moderate, Severe and Profound Learning Difficulties
Practical strategies

The Effective Teacher's Guide to Sensory Impairment and Physical Disability
Practical strategies

The Effective Teacher's Guide to Behavioural, Emotional and Social Difficulties

Practical strategies

Michael Farrell

Routledge
Taylor & Francis Group

LONDON AND NEW YORK

First published 2006
by Routledge
2 Park Square, Milton Park, Abingdon, Oxon OX14 4RN

Simultaneously published in the USA and Canada
by Routledge
270 Madison Ave, New York, NY 10016

Routledge is an imprint of the Taylor & Francis Group

© 2006 Michael Farrell

Typeset in Times New Roman and Gill by
Florence Production Ltd, Stoodleigh, Devon
Printed and bound in Great Britain by
Bell & Bain Ltd, Glasgow

British Library Cataloguing in Publication Data
A catalogue record for this book is available from the British Library

Library of Congress Cataloging in Publication Data
A catalog record has been requested for this book

ISBN10: 0–415–36038–2

ISBN13: 9–78–0–415–36038–8

Contents

List of abbreviations   vi

1   What are BESD?   1

2   Systems approach   17

3   Cognitive approach   29

4   Behavioural approach   41

5   Psychodynamic and related approaches   53

6   Attention deficit hyperactivity disorder (ADHD)   63

7   Conclusion   73

Addresses   81

Bibliography   87

Index   93

Abbreviations

ADHD	attention deficit hyperactivity disorder
BEP	behaviour environment plan
BESD	behavioural, emotional and social difficulties
DfEE	Department for Education and Employment
DfES	Department for Education and Skills
ESPP	Early Support Pilot Programme
IBP	individual behaviour plan
IEP	individual education plan
LEA	local education authority
P4C	Philosophy for Children
PLASC	Pupil Level Annual School Census
PSHCE	personal, social, health and citizenship education
PSP	pastoral support programme
REBT	rational-emotive behavioural therapy
RRS	Reintegration Readiness Scale
SEN	special educational needs
SENCO	special educational needs co-ordinator

Dr Michael Farrell trained as a teacher and as a psychologist at the Institute of Psychiatry and has worked as a head teacher, a lecturer at the Institute of Education, London and as a local education authority inspector. He managed national projects for City University and for the Government Department of Education. Michael Farrell presently works as a special educational consultant. This has involved policy development and training with LEAs, work with voluntary organisations, support to schools in the independent and maintained sectors, and advice to ministries abroad. Among his numerous books, which are translated into European and Asian languages, are:

Key Issues for Primary Schools (Routledge, 1999)

Key Issues for Secondary Schools (Routledge, 2001)

Understanding Special Educational Needs: A Guide for Student Teachers (Routledge, 2003)

Key Issues in Special Education (Routledge, 2005)

Chapter 1

What are BESD?

INTRODUCTION

This chapter sets the book in the context of the 'New Directions in Special Educational Needs' series of which it forms a part. It outlines the contents of the book and describes the proposed readers. I then attempt to define behavioural, emotional and social difficulties (BESD) and describe pupils considered to have BESD. This is done with reference to the *Special Educational Needs Code of Practice* (DfES, 2001a); the guidance, *Data Collection by Type of Special Educational Needs* (DfES, 2003); the legal definition of special educational needs (SEN); and a consideration of the 'separate' implications of behaviour, emotional state and development, and social skills. I also describe so-called 'challenging behaviours', and subsequently touch on the sort of provision from which pupils with BESD appear to benefit.

The chapter considers the limitations of seeking causes of BESD, looks at the factors associated with BESD and considers their prevalence. The issue of inclusion is examined with particular reference to pupils with BESD, looking at social inclusion, the inclusion of pupils already in mainstream schools and the balance of pupils in mainstream and special schools with particular reference to the guidance, *Inclusive Schooling: Children with Special Educational Needs* (DfES, 2001b). Finally, I examine the issues of professionals working together, working with parents and encouraging pupils' involvement.

The place of this book in the New Directions in Special Educational Needs series and an outline of the chapter contents

This book, *The Effective Teacher's Guide to Behavioural, Emotional and Social Difficulties: Practical Strategies*, is part of a 'New Directions in Special Educational Needs' series covering the types of SEN related to those outlined in the *Special Educational Needs Code of Practice* (DfES, 2001a). The series focuses on what works in the education of pupils with SEN. It covers:

- behavioural, emotional and social difficulties;
- learning difficulties (moderate, severe, and profound and multiple learning difficulties);
- specific learning difficulties (dyslexia, dyspraxia, dyscalculia);
- communication and interaction difficulties (speech, language and communication difficulties; autistic spectrum disorder);
- sensory and physical difficulties (visual impairment, hearing impairment, multi-sensory impairment, physical disability).

The present book covers:

Chapter 2: Systems approach

This explains the systems approach and identification and assessment in relation to it. The chapter considers interventions such as using a framework for intervention across a local education authority (LEA), and circle time.

Chapter 3: Cognitive approach

This chapter outlines a cognitive approach. It examines identification and assessment in this perspective. I consider related interventions such as anxiety management and self-talk.

Chapter 4: Behavioural approach

This chapter considers the behavioural approach. It looks at identification and assessment in this approach. I examine several interventions that relate to a behavioural perspective, including modelling and shaping, and several vehicles for behavioural approaches, such as social skills training, and behaviourally focused contracts.

Chapter 5: Psychodynamic approach

In this chapter I look at a psychodynamic approach and at identification and assessment within it. Interventions considered include therapies such as music therapy and play therapy, the potentially cathartic and communicative elements in the curriculum and the use of counselling skills.

Chapter 6: Attention deficit hyperactivity disorder (ADHD)

This chapter seeks to define ADHD and considers its prevalence and possible causes. It explains why ADHD is considered in the *Special Educational Needs Code of Practice* DfES, 2001a) within BESD. I examine how ADHD is identified and assessed. I look at interventions for pupils with ADHD such as minimising classroom distractions and enabling the unobtrusive management of behaviour.

Chapter 7: Conclusion

The final chapter gives an overview of provision, drawing together some of the themes of earlier chapters.

Each chapter has its own introduction and ends with recommended key texts and thinking points. At the end of the book is a list of physical and internet addresses, a bibliography and a combined subject and author index.

Proposed readers

The book is intended particularly for the following readers:

◆ all teachers, special educational needs co-ordinators (SENCOs) and head teachers in mainstream schools and units working with pupils with BESD;
◆ all staff in special schools providing for pupils with BESD;
◆ staff in pupil referral units who have pupils with BESD;
◆ LEA officers with an interest in and/or responsibility for pupils with BESD;
◆ student teachers and newly qualified teachers wishing to gain an understanding of educational provision for pupils with BESD;
◆ teachers and others undergoing continuing professional development;
◆ school advisers and inspectors.

What are BESD?

The Special Educational Needs Code of Practice

As a starting point, the *Special Educational Needs Code of Practice* (DfES, 2001a) provides a basic description of BESD. Pupils with BESD may:

◆ be withdrawn or isolated;
◆ be disruptive and disturbing;
◆ be hyperactive and lacking concentration;
◆ have immature social skills;
◆ present challenging behaviours arising from other complex special needs.
(Chapter 7: section 60, paraphrased)

Possible triggers for intervention at the level of Early Years Action include, 'the practitioner's or parent's concern about a child who, despite receiving appropriate educational experiences . . . presents persistent emotional and/or behaviour difficulties, which are not ameliorated by the behaviour management techniques usually employed in the setting' (4: 21). In the case of Early Years Action Plus in general, the triggers for seeking help outside the school could be that, 'despite receiving an individualised programme and/or concentrated support, the child . . . [has] emotional and behavioural difficulties which substantially or regularly interfere with the child's own learning or that of the group, despite having an individualised behaviour management programme' (4: 31).

In the primary phase, the triggers for School Action could be, 'the teacher's or others' concern, underpinned by evidence, about a child, who despite receiving differentiated learning opportunities . . . presents persistent emotional and behavioural difficulties which are not ameliorated by the behaviour management techniques usually employed by the school' (5: 44). School Action Plus triggers in the primary phase could be that:

despite receiving an individualised programme and/or concentrated support under School Action, the child . . . has emotional or behavioural difficulties which substantially and regularly interfere with the child's own learning or that of the class group, despite having an individualised behaviour management programme.

(5: 56)

Turning to the secondary sector, School Action (6: 51) and School Action Plus triggers (6: 64) are almost identical to those for the primary phase. Regarding the statutory assessment of SEN, when an LEA is deciding whether to carry out an assessment, it should:

seek evidence of any identifiable factors that could impact on learning outcomes including . . . evidence of significant emotional or behavioural difficulties, as indicated by clear recorded examples of withdrawn or disruptive behaviour; a marked and persistent inability to concentrate; signs that the child experiences considerable frustration or distress in relation to their learning difficulties; difficulties in establishing and maintaining balanced relationships with fellow pupils or with adults; and any other evidence of a significant delay in the development of life and social skills.

(7: 43)

In the light of evidence about what the *Code* calls the child's 'learning difficulty', but which in fact refers to the child's SEN, the LEA should consider the action taken and particularly should ask whether, 'the school has implemented its policy on pastoral care and guidance and sought external advice to meet any social, emotional or behavioural difficulties' (7: 49). The *Code* also notes that, 'Many children with mental health problems, though by no means all, may also be recognised as children with emotional and behavioural difficulties' (10: 27).

The guidance, Data Collection by Type of Special Educational Needs

A further description of BESD is provided in the guidance, *Data Collection by Type of Special Educational Needs*, connected with the Pupil Level Annual School Census (PLASC) (DfES, 2003) (www.dfes.gov.uk/sen). The Department for Education and Skills (DfES) sent original draft descriptions to a sample of schools, LEAs and voluntary organisations and amended them in the light of the comments received. Pupils with BESD tend not to respond to the usual provision of a school that works with most pupils. The guidance points out that the behaviours persist in spite of the implementation of an effective school behaviour policy and an effective curriculum for personal and social education. Pupils cover the 'full range of ability' and the degree of severity of BESD is seen as a 'continuum' (p. 4).

More specifically, the guidance describes behaviour on the continuum of BESD. At the 'milder end' of the continuum, pupils may:

◆ have difficulties with social interaction, finding it difficult to work in a group or cope in unstructured time;
◆ have poor concentration;

◆ have outbursts of temper;
◆ be verbally aggressive to peers and adults.

(p. 4, paraphrased)

Other pupils, one assumes from the middle part of the supposed continuum, although the guidance does not make this explicit, may, 'provoke peers and be confrontational or openly defiant and sometimes physically aggressive towards peers and adults' (p. 4). They are, 'often off task and have a very short concentration span'. Also, 'Their self-esteem is low and they find it hard to accept praise or to take responsibility for their behaviour' (p. 4). Yet other pupils, presumably towards the severe end of the continuum, 'may not be able to function at all in group situations and exhibit persistent and frequent violent behaviour which requires physical intervention' (p. 4).

The continuum outlined above focuses on pupils whose behaviour is usually obvious and noticeable because it is disruptive. However, as the guidance recognises, other pupils are withdrawn, quiet and uncommunicative, and may still show, like disruptive pupils, signs of low self-esteem, underachievement and inappropriate social interaction.

Of pupils with ADHD it is stated rather obviously that they may have reduced attention and may be impulsive or hyperactive.

Behavioural, emotional and social difficulties and the legal definition of SEN

Many types of SEN can be better understood by examining them in the context of the legal definition of SEN in the Education Act 1996. The Act provides a layered definition in which a 'difficulty in learning' or a 'disability' may lead to a 'learning difficulty', which may call for special educational provision to be made, therefore constituting an SEN. But BESD are not as well illuminated as some other types of SEN by the Act.

From a behavioural perspective, problematic behaviour and poor social skills can be explained by saying the pupil has not learned acceptable behaviour or age-appropriate social skills. There has been a 'difficulty in learning' these skills of such significance that it may be considered a 'learning difficulty' constituting an SEN. The educational response that would fit this perspective would involve unlearning the inappropriate skills and learning appropriate skills. Modern behavioural approaches are somewhat more sophisticated than this and cognitive and other possible factors are taken into account. Other perspectives, such as systems and psychotherapeutic, also inform the understanding of BESD.

From another viewpoint, some forms of BESD, for example ADHD, may be considered to have a psycho-physiological basis that could suggest that it be considered as a 'disability'. The disability might be such that it could be considered a 'learning difficulty' that may in turn call for special educational provision, making it an SEN. Physiological bases for BESD however are contested and also the notion of disability in the context of the Education Act 1996 seems to apply more securely to disabilities and impairments that are more obviously physical in their manifestations, such as visual impairment hearing impairment and physical disability.

Despite these limitations, the legal definition at least reminds educators that BESD are considered a special *educational* need.

Separate consideration of behaviour, emotions and social skills

So, if the notion of 'difficulty in learning', 'disability' and 'learning difficulty' offer limited insight into how BESD link with the educational part of SEN, what can constitute a suitable understanding that makes stronger connections with the education of children with BESD?

Broadly, it is that behaviour, emotions and social development all influence learning and access to learning. Difficulties with behaviour, emotions and social development can all inhibit learning and access to learning. In the current jargon, they can form barriers to learning. They are often interrelated but considering them for a moment separately makes it possible to illustrate their impact on learning.

A pupil's behaviour may be very withdrawn (this may be interpreted also as evidence of poor social skills). Contact with other children, teachers and adults is therefore limited with obvious negative effects on learning, including acquiring social skills. The pupil may avoid attending school for long periods. Alternatively, a pupil's behaviour may be disruptive and confrontational. While the pupil engages in such behaviour, he is unlikely to be absorbed in lessons and his learning will suffer. He may also of course disrupt the learning of other pupils.

The emotional development and the emotional state of a pupil may inhibit learning. Low self-esteem, the experience of emotional trauma or emotional instability may affect concentration, sociability and school attendance. The social development of a pupil may be limited. This may mean that the social skills necessary to play a constructive role in the school community, with all the potential benefits to learning that this brings, are hindered. It can be seen then that BESD are possible indicators of poor learning and development themselves. Also, they can act as barriers to learning, despite the efforts of teachers and others.

Challenging behaviour

As stated earlier, the *Special Educational Needs Code of Practice* (DfES, 2001a) provides a basic description of BESD. This includes that pupils with BESD may 'present challenging behaviours arising from other complex special needs' (7: 60).

The term 'challenging behaviour' is sometimes used as a euphemism for BESD, while at other times it refers to a range of behaviours that particularly stretch the resources and skills of teachers and others. It is this second interpretation that this section explores. One definition is that challenging behaviour is behaviour:

> which is socially unacceptable and significantly blocks learning. Its intensity, duration or frequency is such that the safety of the person exhibiting the behaviour or the safety of others is at risk. Such behaviour is likely to limit access to community facilities or completely prohibit it.
>
> (Farrell, 2003, p. 29)

There is not always agreement about what constitutes challenging behaviour any more than there is uniform consensus about BESD more generally. In part this relates to varying standards of what is considered acceptable, influenced by factors such as social class, culture, different chronological ages and developmental 'ages' of children, and different settings.

Examples of challenging behaviour are likely to include:

◆ self-injury;
◆ injury to others;
◆ damage to the surroundings;
◆ severe non-compliance;
◆ stereotyped movement or speech;
◆ faecal smearing;
◆ pica (habitually eating substances other than food, such as paper or dirt);
◆ unacceptable sexual behaviour, such as public masturbation or exposing the genitals to others;
◆ persistent screaming.

In some instances, challenging behaviour is associated with a particular syndrome, such as Lesch-Nyhan syndrome, which is linked with self-injurious behaviour and sometimes violence to others, spitting and vomiting. Often a child with Tourette's syndrome, a severe, chronic tic disorder, exhibits challenging behaviour. The syndrome manifests itself in early childhood with motor tics and later includes motor and vocal tics, which in some cases involve repetitive verbal or gestural obscenities or the repetition of overheard words and the persistent imitation of the movements of others (Carol and Robertson, 2000).

Provision for pupils with BESD

Later chapters of the book explore provision for pupils with BESD in the light of different perspectives, including behavioural, cognitive and psychodynamic perspectives. The purpose of the present section is to indicate something more about the nature of BESD by touching on the interventions that are used when educating pupils with BESD.

As a starting point, the *Special Educational Needs Code of Practice* (DfES, 2001a) provides a basic description of provision from which pupils with BESD may benefit. They may require:

◆ counselling;
◆ help with developing social competence and emotional maturity;
◆ help in adjusting to school expectations and routines;
◆ help in acquiring the skills to interact positively with peers and adults;
◆ specialised behaviour and cognitive approaches;
◆ re-channelling or re-focusing to diminish repetitive or self-injurious behaviours;
◆ provision of class and school systems that control or censure negative or difficult behaviours and encourage positive behaviours;
◆ provision of a safe and supportive environment.

(7: 60, modified)

Guidance connected with the PLASC (DfES, 2003) (www.dfes.gov.uk/sen) indicates that pupils should only be recorded as having BESD, 'if additional educational provision is being made to help them to access the curriculum' (p. 4).

More specifically, pupils with BESD can benefit from certain provision from the school as a community and from teachers in particular. These vary in different circumstances and are affected by the main types of behaviour (e.g. aggressive, withdrawn, hyperactive) concerned. Provision might include:

◆ teachers having the commitment and resilience to provide and maintain clear boundaries for aggressive and abusive behaviour;
◆ curricular opportunities for pupils to express and release emotions through subjects such as art, music, physical education and drama;
◆ the direct and indirect teaching of appropriate behaviour and social skills through the general running of the school, staff example, personal and social education (as a given for all pupils) and specific interventions such as social skills training;
◆ giving the time and commitment to ensuring that the pupil has at least one adult with whom he enjoys a trusting relationship and with whom he can talk issues through.

A further dimension is necessary for some pupils with BESD that is outside the usual range of skills of the teacher and for which specialist support may be needed. This may include:

◆ counselling and, for a few, psychotherapy;
◆ family support and counselling and, for a few, family therapy;
◆ music therapy, drama therapy, art therapy and play therapy;
◆ the development of emotional literacy;
◆ residential provision;
◆ medication for a tiny minority.

With such provision, the pupil is more likely to benefit from the education that the school offers for all pupils and to make better progress reaching higher standards of achievement, including personal and social development and self-esteem. A virtuous spiral might then be started in which the pupil begins to achieve better educationally, with positive effects on behaviour and personal and social development, which in turn contribute to the pupil being more able to take advantage of ordinary educational provision.

Causal factors and associated aspects

A further understanding of pupils with BESD might be expected from an examination of the apparent causes of BESD. However, there is great difficulty in trying to convincingly relate the causes of BESD directly to particular kinds of behaviour, emotional difficulties or impaired social skills. For clarity of exposition, apparent causes and related provision are sometimes linked. For example, a view that some behavioural difficulties may be brought about by poor behaviours being learned and appropriate behaviours not being learned can be linked to a behavioural approach that concentrates on unlearning unsuitable behaviour and learning appropriate behaviour. But few today believe that a behavioural explanation (or any other single explanation) is enough and behavioural explanations, for example, often incorporate cognitive insights. In practice other approaches are also often used.

Even to speak of causes can elevate to an unjustifiable prominence factors that are simply often associated with BESD but that can rarely be claimed unequivocally to have caused the BESD.

Factors associated with BESD include:

◆ traumatic childhood experiences;
◆ a family background that is fractious or very insecure;
◆ poor models of behaviour, such as family violence;
◆ a family history of BESD.

However, it will immediately be recognised that there are children for whom such factors are all too evident but who do not experience BESD. Similarly, there are pupils who experience BESD for whom such factors are not evident and indeed for whom no convincing explanation is forthcoming.

In practical terms, it is most useful to bear possible causative factors in mind when looking at a pupil's background history, perhaps as a clue to explaining some of the BESD. But in reality the probability that there are multiple, interactive causes, and some causes that may never become known to educators and others, suggests that a search for definitive causes and explanations is unlikely to be very fruitful. Accordingly, a pragmatic approach to provision is suggested while at the same time taking note of the explanations provided by various approaches (systems, cognitive, behavioural, psychodynamic) and what works in schools that are successful in educating pupils with BESD.

Prevalence of BESD

If one is as clear as possible about what BESD are and from what provision pupils considered to have BESD might benefit, it might be thought that it is easier to determine prevalence. But determining the prevalence of BESD is as contentious as seeking its apparent cause is difficult.

Many SENCOs will have had to resolve a situation in which a teacher with poor skills in managing children is convinced that most of the pupils in the class have BESD when their behaviour is more accurately explained as a reaction to poor teaching and pupil management. But the school has to work through such situations to gain an idea of which pupils, if any, do not respond to what the school normally offers to support and encourage good behaviour, good social skills and emotional security among pupils.

Pupils with BESD are by definition those who do not respond to what the school normally provides. A further check on the over-identification of pupils supposedly having BESD is the involvement of outside specialists who enjoy a wider perspective than the one school, often having responsibilities covering 20 or 30 schools. Such specialists as members of the LEA behaviour support team can help the school to recognise the degree of severity of the BESD in this wider context as well as offering practical advice and help as necessary.

A further filtering system is the procedures for School Action, School Action Plus, statutory assessment criteria and the review of statements of SEN and their discontinuation. Therefore to think in terms of definite numbers of pupils per school or in percentages is in a sense unhelpful. There are too many other factors to take into account. As a general rule, the numbers of pupils considered to have BESD should be as small as the school can make it given the need to secure the effective education of all children.

Regarding pupils identified as having, 'behaviour, emotional and social difficulties', in England in January 2004 (DfES, 2004, table 9), there were 94,320 (26.8 per cent) at School Action Plus and a further 32,570 (13.8 per cent) with statements of SEN.

The specific figures for ordinary primary and secondary schools and for special schools are as follows. In primary schools, 44,120 of pupils with BESD were at School Action Plus (20.2 per cent of all pupils at School Action Plus in primary schools) and 8,440 had statements of SEN (12.3 per cent of all pupils with statements in primary schools). In secondary schools, the number was greater for both School Action Plus and statements, being 49,960 at School Action Plus (38 per cent) and 11,980 with statements of SEN (15.3 per cent). In special schools, where it is much less usual for pupils *not* to have statements of SEN, there were only 240 pupils at School Action Plus (14.6 per cent) and 12,150 with statements of SEN (13.7 per cent). The figures for special schools included pupils attending maintained and non-maintained special schools but excluded pupils in independent special schools or maintained hospital schools.

Inclusion and BESD

One understanding of inclusion is that it aims to encourage schools to reconsider their structure, teaching approaches, pupil grouping and use of support so that the school responds to the perceived needs of all its pupils. Teachers, collaborating closely, seek opportunities to look at new ways of involving all pupils and to draw on experimentation and reflection. There should be planned access to a broad and balanced curriculum developed from its foundations as a curriculum for all pupils.

One view of inclusion is that it concerns educating more pupils in mainstream schools and fewer, or none, in special schools and other venues regarded as segregating. However, it may be argued that special schools can also be inclusive (Farrell, 2000). Indeed, the Qualifications and Curriculum Authority has characterised inclusion as, 'securing appropriate opportunities for learning, assessment and qualifications to enable the full and effective participation of all pupils in the process of learning' (Wade, 1999).

Three aspects of inclusion in relation to BESD

Social inclusion

Social inclusion was the theme of two government circulars, *10/99* (DfEE, 1999a) and *11/99* (DfEE, 1999b). *Circular 10/99* highlights the need to provide for pupils in school rather than physically excluding them through short-term or permanent exclusions. One way of cutting down such exclusion from school is seeking to reduce disaffection, in particular, among pupils in known high-risk categories. Among these categories are pupils with SEN who may develop challenging behaviour and pupils whose attainments tend to be very low. The links between these pupils and pupils with BESD will be apparent although the two groups are by no means identical. *Circular 10/99* suggests that approaches for pupils at risk should include early intervention, careful planning and whole school strategies. School-based pastoral support programmes (PSPs) were to be developed with the help of external services for pupils at serious risk of permanent exclusion or of being drawn into criminal behaviour. For pupils already having individual education plans (IEPs), these should be made to encompass the features of a PSP.

Normally, a PSP will have been put into operation and will have failed before the school resorts to exclusion. Once a pupil is excluded, the head teacher and the LEA should plan for his or her reintegration into school-based education. It will be seen that the guidance of *Circular 10/99* includes identifying groups of pupils who appear from past experience to be at risk of exclusion. The school had to take care that in identifying such pupils they were not contributing to a self-fulfilling prophesy by over-expecting disaffection where there might be none. The circular then suggested strategies to avoid exclusion and explained documentation that would indicate that the school had consulted outside specialists and had not been precipitous in excluding a pupil. Finally, it set expectations that plans would be made for pupils' reintegration.

Circular 11/99 concerned the LEA's role in supporting pupils at risk of exclusion or who had been excluded. It emphasises that pupils excluded for more than three weeks should get a suitable full-time suitable alternative education. LEAs and other agencies should work to reduce exclusions in line with a national target. The LEA must consider compelling school attendance through legal remedies and should support schools that have pupils with PSPs.

Including pupils with SEN already in mainstream school

A second aspect of inclusion is that of including pupils with SEN who are already in mainstream schools. This approach seems to be the purpose of documents seeking to encourage this kind of inclusion, such as the *Index for Inclusion* (Booth *et al.*, 2000). The document concerns the inclusion of all those connected with the school, adults as well as children, not only pupils with SEN.

Developing an inclusive ethos and inclusive approaches may increase the school's capacity to include pupils with BESD who are presently not in mainstream or who otherwise might be considered to be better placed in another setting, such as a special school or unit. This leads to a consideration of the third aspect of inclusion, the balance of pupils in mainstream schools and other settings such as special schools.

The balance of pupils in mainstream and special schools

The expression, 'full inclusion', as it applies to pupils with SEN, indicates the view that all pupils with SEN should be educated in mainstream schools. A range of provision in which pupils with SEN could be educated (such as mainstream school, special school, pupil referral unit, home tuition) would not be acceptable. It would be better to have increased support and resources in mainstream schools in proportion to the severity and complexity of SEN (e.g. Gartner and Lipsky, 1989). Full inclusion is not the position of the government in England nor is it that of any of the major political parties in opposition at the time of writing.

The document, *Inclusive Schooling: Children with Special Educational Needs* (DfES, 2001b), gives statutory guidance on the framework for inclusion. The Special Educational Needs and Disability Act 2001 is said to deliver a 'strengthened right to a mainstream education for children with special educational needs' (4: 1) by amending the Education Act 1996.

Concerning the nature of the proposed 'right' to inclusion, it is clear that this is constrained. This is indicated by the *Inclusive Schooling* document referring to a 'strengthened right' to mainstream education (1: 4). The right (if that is the correct word) is partial. The extent of the right can be seen from the commensurate duties that are placed on others in connection with the 'right'.

As a result of the Special Educational Needs and Disability Act 2001, the Education Act 1996 section 316(3) was amended to read:

> If a statement is maintained under section 324 for the child, he must be educated in a mainstream school unless that is incompatible with:
>
> ◆ the wishes of his parent, or
> ◆ the provision of efficient education for other children.

The use of the word 'must' in the above section of the Act indicates the duty of the LEA and others that corresponds to the 'right' to be educated in the mainstream. If the education of a child with SEN is incompatible with the efficient education of other pupils, mainstream education can only be refused if there are no reasonable steps that can be taken to prevent the incompatibility. But it may not be possible to take steps to prevent a child's inclusion being incompatible with the efficient education of others. This may arise for example when a child's behaviour systematically, persistently and significantly threatens the safety or impedes the learning of others. It may also arise where the teacher, even with other support, has to spend a greatly disproportionate amount of time with the child in relation to the rest of the class.

The 'rights' are further affected when one considers a particular school rather than the generic concept of 'mainstream'. Parents may express a preference for a particular mainstream school to be named in their child's statement of SEN. In this case, schedule 27 of the Education Act 1996 requires the LEA to name the parents' preferred choice of school in the child's statement unless any of three conditions apply. These are:

1 the school cannot provide for the needs of the child;
2 the child's inclusion at the school would be incompatible with the efficient education of other pupils;
3 the child's inclusion at the school would be incompatible with the efficient use of resources.

It will be seen that there is no comprehensive 'right' of attendance at a main-stream school, but that the rights of the parents of a child with SEN are balanced against the 'rights' of the parents of children who do not have SEN and against other factors. It is in this context that provision – what works best for pupils with BESD – should be understood.

Professionals working closely together

Professionals involved with children with BESD may include the teacher, general practitioner, school nurse, school medical officer, the Child and Adolescent Mental Health Service, LEA behaviour support staff, educational psychologist, educational welfare officer, social worker and others. Each may have different professional perspectives and different levels of experience concerning BESD. Professional trust is essential but is difficult to build up where staff turnover is very high. For multi-professional working to be practicable, clear lines of communication are necessary as is a structure that demarcates responsibility without being too constraining.

Early Years Development and Childcare Partnerships use interagency planning to bring together early years education and social care. Those working in health action zones and education action zones have tried to co-ordinate action on social disadvantage and social support for pupils with SEN. SEN regional partnerships have encouraged discussions and joint planning between education, health and social services on some topics. Aspects of the Excellence in Cities programme included encouraging school-based learning support units working with pupils at risk of exclusion from school to work with learning mentors and out-of-school support services. The Sure Start initiative offered the opportunity to interrelate family policy and the early identification and support of pupils with SEN.

In 2003, an Early Support Pilot Programme (ESPP) was designed to develop good service provision and to support development in various areas, including the co-ordination of multi-agency support for families and partnership across agencies and geographical boundaries. This involved joint work between the DfES and others such as the Royal National Institute for the Blind, the Royal National Institute for the Deaf and the National Children's Bureau (www.earlysupport. org.uk). See also the DfES website (www.dfes.gov.uk/sen), the Department of Health website (www.doh.gov.uk) or the National Children's Bureau website (www.ncb.org.uk).

Related to joint professional working, a National Children's Trust Framework was announced in 2001 intended to develop new standards across the National Health Service and social services for children and encourage partnership between agencies. Children's Trusts were subsequently seen as seeking to integrate local education, social care and some health services (through the Health Act 1999, section 31) for children and young people and incorporate an integrated commissioning strategy. The LEA will include potentially all education functions, including SEN, the education welfare service and educational psychology. Children's social services will include assessment and services for children 'in need'. Community and acute health services will include locally provided and commissioned child and adolescent mental health services and could also include speech and language therapy, health visiting and occupational therapy services

concerned with children and families. (Primary Care Trusts will be able to dele-
gate functions into the Children's Trust and will be able to pool funds with the
local authority.)

Children's Trusts can also include other services such as Connexions, Youth
Offending teams and Sure Start. Other local partners such as the police, voluntary organisations, housing services and leisure services can be involved.
Children's Trusts are expected to sit within local authorities, reporting to the
director of children's services who in turn will report through the chief executive
to the local councillors. The Children's Trusts will commission services and may
provide these directly or by contracts through public, private or voluntary sector
organisations.

The resulting integration of service provision is expected to be reflected in
features including: co-located services such as Children's Centres and extended
schools; multi-disciplinary teams and a key worker system; a common assessment
framework across services; information-sharing systems across services; joint
training; and effective arrangements for safeguarding children. The intention is to
integrate key children's services within a single organisational focus, preferably
through Children's Trusts, which it was envisaged would exist in most areas by
2006. Bids for 35 'Pathfinder' Trusts were approved in 2003, funded to 2006
(www.doh.gov.uk/nsf/children/index.htm).

Working with parents

Working closely with parents is an aspiration of all schools and a continuing
theme in government guidance. The *Special Educational Needs Code of Practice*
(DfES, 2001a) devotes a chapter to 'Working in partnership with parents' and
specific guidance on seeking to understand what parents might need is available
(e.g. Greenwood, 2002). The perspectives on BESD covered in later chapters
assume that parents are as fully involved as is practicable. A joint systems
approach, for example, may focus on the two systems of family and school.

The school's support of parents may include:

◆ contacting parents when there is good news to impart as well as when there
   is bad;
◆ providing information about BESD and practical strategies for coping;
◆ putting parents in touch with support groups locally and nationally;
◆ making school premises available for various activities such as a parent support
   group;
◆ having displays of literature such as leaflets;
◆ being a 'one stop' point of contact for other services;
◆ holding information evenings at which parents can see what their child has
   been doing in school, perhaps with a focus such as 'the internet' or 'outdoor
   pursuits'.

A model for collaborating with parents in order to help pupils experiencing
difficulties at school is suggested by Hornby (2003, p. 131). It distinguishes
between what it is considered parents 'need' and what it can reasonably be
expected they can contribute.

Parents *needs* are considered to be for communication with the school (which all parents need); liaison such as that taking place at parent–teacher meetings (which most parents need); education such as parents' workshops (which many need); and support such as counselling (which some need).

Parents' *contributions* are considered as information, for example about the child's strengths (which all parents can provide); collaboration, for example with behaviour programmes or supporting a pupil's IEPs (to which most parents could contribute); resources, such as being a classroom aid (to which many could contribute); and helping develop policy, for example being a parent governor of the school (to which some could contribute).

The model leaves open the exact interpretation of what the expressions 'most', 'many' and 'some' might mean and schools will bring their own judgements to bear on, for example, whether it is reasonable to expect 'many' parents to contribute at a level suggested by being a classroom aid. Nevertheless the basic structure of the model with a graduated view of the parents' proposed needs and contributions is a helpful one.

Pupils' views

Lewis (2004) lists some aspects of methods relevant to chronologically young children or 'developmentally young' children. These include:

◆ permit or encourage 'don't know' responses and requests for clarification;
◆ stress not knowing the events or views of the child to counter the child's assumption that the adult knows the answer (the child tends to be more suggestible if the adult has credibility and rapport with the child);
◆ use statements rather than questions to trigger fuller responses from children;
◆ aim for an uninterrupted narrative.

(Lewis, 2004, pp. 4–6 paraphrased)

With regard specifically to pupils with BESD, some approaches may seem to encourage participation more than others although this can be deceptive. For example, a behavioural approach might appear to discourage pupil participation because it rewards or sanctions a child's behaviour according to social norms. However, such approaches often involve the pupil in discussions about aspects of behaviour that might be an agreed focus for change; in setting negotiated targets; and in evaluating progress. Also, behavioural approaches often involve cognitive elements such as self-monitoring and are also used in eclectic conjunction with interventions with a systems or a psychodynamic basis.

The *Special Educational Needs Code of Practice* (DfES, 2001a, especially Chapter 3) encourages pupil participation and seeks to involve pupils with BESD in the development and evaluations of IEPs and behaviour support plans where possible. A balance is sought between encouraging participation and over-burdening the pupil when he may not have sufficient experience and knowledge to make judgements without support.

THINKING POINT

Readers may wish to consider with reference to a particular school:

◆   the effectiveness of procedures for seeking a commonly held understanding of BESD, such as discussion, consultation with the SENCO and observation.

KEY TEXTS

Ayers, H. and Prytys, C. (2002) *An A to Z Practical Guide to Emotional and Behavioural Difficulties*, London, David Fulton Publishers.

This reference book includes entries on topics reflecting the behavioural, psychodynamic, cognitive and systems approaches and ADHD and often includes references for further reading.

Farrell, M. (2003) *The Special Education Handbook* (3rd edn), London, David Fulton Publishers.

Particular entries that may be useful include: 'art therapy' 'behaviour modification', 'behaviour therapy', 'challenging behaviour', 'circle time', 'cognitive approaches', 'counselling', 'emotional, behavioural and social difficulties', 'psychoanalysis and psychotherapy', 'social skills', 'token economy' and 'residential therapy'. Appendices summarise legislation and related reports and consultative documents from the 'Warnock report' to the present day; selected regulations from 1981 to the present; and selected circulars and circular letters from 1981 to the present including the *Special Educational Needs Code of Practice* of 2001 and the Special Educational Needs and Disability Act 2001. There are summaries of *Circular 1/94: The Education of Children with Emotional and Behavioural Difficulties*; *Circular 10/99: Social Inclusion: Pupil Support*; and *Circular 11/99: Social Inclusion: The LEA Role in Pupil Support*.

Chapter 2

Systems approach

INTRODUCTION

This chapter introduces and explains systems approaches to BESD, touching first on family therapy then examining a school systems approach and a joint systems approach to the school and the child's family. I look briefly at how supposed causal factors of BESD are viewed. I then consider identification and assessment in relation to this approach, including sociometric methods and circular questioning. I examine various interventions informed by a systems approach concentrating on: a framework for intervention across an LEA; group work, circle time and Circle of Friends; interventions by outside specialists; and school and family liaison.

What is a systems approach?

A systems approach

A systems approach is not synonymous with having effective management and accountability systems that operate at LEA and school levels. Rather, a systems perspective concerns viewing behaviour in relation to the contexts in which it occurs. The term, 'ecosystemic perspective' is often currently used in relation to systems approaches (e.g. Ayers and Prytys, 2002, p. 94). Based on systems theory and family therapy, the ecosystemic perspective is an interactional approach covering similar ground. In this chapter a systems view refers to an approach that looks to systems in the family and the school to inform approaches to pupils that might in other approaches be considered to have BESD.

Family therapy

Family therapy (Dallo and Draper, 2000) refers to various group therapy approaches in which the therapist sees all family members together. One assumption of this perspective is that where there is an apparent problem, which might appear to be located in a particular family member, for example a child considered to have BESD, the problem in fact is better seen as being within the family as a whole.

The approach is enabling in that family members are encouraged to communicate with each other and seek solutions to the problem as it appears. The therapist may offer different strategies to encourage family members to behave, think and feel differently. Various 'schools' of family therapy have developed, such as the structural family therapy model and strategic family therapy, as well as systemic family therapy (e.g. Gurman and Messer, 2003, Chapter 11).

The school in a systems approach

Systems approaches reflect, 'a view of individual behaviour which takes account of the context in which it occurs' (Dowling and Osborne, 1994, p. 3). A systems view may be distinguished from a linear model, which seeks a rationale to explain the apparent causes and effects of behaviour. The systems perspective regards behaviour as existing within a context, indicating an interactional and holistic view of behaviour rather than an individual one.

The idea of circular causality is used to suggest that sequences of interactions contribute to the continuation of a 'problem'. In this light, it becomes more relevant to ask *how* a problem occurs than to ask *why* it happens (p. 5). If someone chooses to 'punctuate' the circle of interaction by focusing on a point in the cycle this can give the impression of a linear cause and effect, which may be deceptive. For example, in a school, there may be a cycle of interaction that perpetuates a pupil and a teacher being in regular conflict. The teacher may punctuate the circle at the point of a pupil's perceived rude and unco-operative behaviour in class and see the problem as predominantly being within the pupil. The pupil may punctuate the circle at the point of the teacher's behaviour towards him and see the problem as being the teacher's perceived negative and demeaning attitude. Neither pupil nor teacher is 'correct' in any absolute sense, in part because there is no absolute sense in which behaviour is evaluated.

Such a view might immediately pose a difficulty for the teacher who is uncomfortable in being expected to assume that the child in her charge has an equally valid perspective of a situation as the teacher herself. It might be interpreted as an example of the erosion of authority and order. But further reflection might suggest that, unless a child's perspective is taken into account, it may be more difficult than otherwise to reach a solution to what are perceived by the teacher and the school as intractable behaviour difficulties. It is not a matter of the child being right and the teacher wrong. It is more a matter of the teacher and others giving the child an opportunity to express the situation from his point of view and seeking to understand it.

Another feature of systems approaches is the concept of the coherence of a system and the extent to which its pieces fit together in a way that is balanced internally and externally in relation to its environment. For example, there may be self-regulating aspects of dysfunctional individual behaviour in the context of a school system. It has been suggested that in this way aspects of a school system may sustain antisocial behaviour. Again this may be difficult for a school to consider or accept as it can appear, to hard-pressed senior managers and others, to be blaming the school for what to them might seem to be the obvious intractability of some pupils. But again further consideration may reveal examples of some aspects of school procedure and routine that might unintentionally be making compliance more difficult for some pupils and lead to a realisation that such routines could be fine-tuned without eroding what is viewed as acceptable school discipline.

Joint systems approaches: the school and the family

Strategies that are seen as being 'systems approaches' sometimes seem to set school system explanations against family system explanations or joint school–family explanations. For example McNamara and Moreton (2001) write that trends in school improvement initiatives have meant, 'that for some schools and LEAs the focus for explanations of poor behaviour has moved away from socio-economic factors and towards classrooms and whole school systems explanations' (p. v). The authors then mention behaviours that teachers find difficult to manage being accepted as 'classroom bound' and therefore related to the curriculum and class-room interpersonal relationships, 'as opposed to the home background' (p. vi). This highlights the aspect of a school systems approach that is careful not to assume 'within child' explanations, but it does not seem to give sufficient credence to the potential of family systems to influence a child's behaviour, or to seek to link the two systems.

Certainly, it may be difficult to determine the boundaries of any particular system but the idea that 'home' and 'school' describe two particular systems is perhaps not too difficult to accept as a working position. A particularly interesting development of a systems approach is that of seeking to understand both the child's family and the school as systems and to develop ways of taking account of the interrelationships between them. An early description of such an approach is to be found in *The Family and the School: A Joint Systems Approach to Problems with Children*, originally published in 1985 (Dowling and Osborne, 1994).

The importance of the wider context is reflected in the fact that both the family and the school are seen as 'open systems', that is, 'systems that cannot be viewed without reference to their influence on the environment in which they exist' (p. 6). Family and the school are seen as closely interlinked over a considerable time period and this 'reciprocal influence' determines how the two systems view one another.

Common elements shared by school and family systems have been suggested, including their hierarchical organisation, rules, culture (including the ethos of an organisation) and belief systems. To take the example of hierarchical organisation in a school, it has been suggested that the organisational structure may influence the perception and behaviour of pupils in a way that leads to them being seen as problematical by those seeking to maintain the structure. Similarly in families, it is considered important that there is a responsible adult 'in charge' and that he or she establishes consistent rules and communicates these to children. This helps children to feel secure and to understand the consequences of any rule-breaking (p. 8).

Clearly both schools and families have rules of some kind, although in a family they may not always be as explicitly stated as in many schools, where it is considered beneficial that rules are made clear and public and the subject of whole-school policies. The particular rules within a family and within a school may differ but the underlying fact that there are rules represents at least some common ground.

The culture of a school relates to its ethos, which can be a slippery concept and something that is sometimes easier to feel and recognise than to articulate. It is suggested in the way that things are almost unconsciously done in the school. (For further discussion of ethos, including a brief outline of some early research into school ethos, see Farrell *et al.*, 1995, pp. 82–3.) In a similar way, the family has its own culture and implicit expectations of the ways in which things are done.

Perhaps in the case of belief systems, the systems are more explicit in families and schools where religious beliefs are involved. But the notion of belief systems is much wider than religious beliefs and encompasses the sometimes subtle and implicit beliefs and values that help determine day-to-day interaction and behaviour.

The aims of a joint systems approach to school and family have been summarised as:

♦ facilitating communication between school, staff and family members;
♦ clarifying differences in the perception of the problem by focusing on how it occurs rather than why it happens;
♦ negotiating commonly agreed goals; and
♦ beginning to explore specific steps towards change.

(Dowling and Osborne, 1994, p. 15)

Causal factors

In a systems approach, causal factors are not related to supposed unconscious processes, or to dysfunctional social perceptions and thinking, or to the learning of unsuitable behaviour. They are considered to be part of the cycle of interaction that takes place within the school and the home and between the two systems. The notion of direct linear cause is therefore challenged.

Identification and assessment in this approach

If usual notions of causation are challenged in a systems approach, then identifying pupils with BESD is also given a rather different slant than in some perspectives. This is because the initial assumption is not that some problem lies predominantly within the pupil that has to be identified before remedial or compensatory action can be taken. It is rather that what is interpreted as a pupil 'difficulty' can be understood in terms of systems and the implications of this are what should be identified and explored. A child or young person might be referred to as 'disturbing' rather than 'disturbed' to at the very least signal more clearly, than might otherwise be the case, the involvement of someone else doing the describing. It will be seen that the emphasis shifts then from seeking explanations 'within' the pupil to seeking explanations for BESD in the school as a system and elsewhere. Indeed, using a systems approach might lead one to use such expressions as BESD with particular care to the extent that the term 'behavioural, emotional and social *difficulty*' can presuppose that the 'difficulty' lies within the pupil.

Just as identification implies recognising aspects of the systems that appear to be influencing the problem context, so assessment involves a broad evaluation of the problematic situation. This might be a case of conflict between the pupil and the teacher, so evidence of the attitudes, views, feelings and behaviour of the pupil and the teacher (and any others involved) is gathered. Among approaches supporting this are those derived from sociometry and the technique of circular questioning.

Sociometry is a theory and a set of practices developed by Jacob Moreno to reveal the social interactions and social dynamics in a group. Each member of the group is given a sociometric test in the form of a rating scale in which each person expresses likes and dislikes of other members of the group. Specific questions might apply to different circumstances such as with whom the member of the group would like to work, spend time with after school and so on. The results are used to make a sociogram, which visually represents group relationships such as isolated pupils and very popular pupils. Sociometric assessment might be used to gather and collate information from other pupils in the class or classes in which difficulties arise. (Frederickson and Cline, 2002, pp. 437–9 provide examples.)

Circular questioning is another assessment technique that can help to gather some of the information and data about perceptions that appear to influence the situation. It explores the connectedness between people and also the links between their beliefs and their behaviour. As well as being a way of gathering information, circular questioning can influence the way that participants view a situation. This, to the extent that it might allow participants to begin to explore different ways of perceiving a situation, can have the effect of an intervention. Circular questioning may be used to capture some of the interactions taking place between different pupils and different aspects of their environment (such as the school, class, groups, home and community). It may involve a small group comprising the pupil, parents, teacher and others in which each is asked to focus on the thoughts, emotions and behaviour of the others and how these might interact.

Interventions

A general theme of interventions

Interventions in a systems approach generally seek to define the problem as it appears in more precise terms than those in which it may initially be seen and expressed. For example, if a child is seen as 'difficult', an initial step might be to try to specify what it is that the child does that is seen as difficult. Observations and recording of the behaviour of a child, for example by a teacher, may contribute to this initial outlining of the perceived problem.

Next, an attempt is made to express the problem in terms of the interactions that are associated with it. What leads to the problem? What follows it? What appears to sustain it? Who else is involved? What in detail is the context? Goals may be considered and agreed in relation to what participants want in the future.

A framework for intervention

This section describes a framework for intervention outlined by Daniels and Williams (2000), which draws on elements of psychology, sociology and general management theory and is essentially a systematic interactional approach to addressing behaviour problems at different levels. It initially concentrates on behaviour environment plans (BEPs) aimed at school and classroom factors and later on developing additional individual behaviour plans (IBPs).

Behaviour in Schools: A Framework for Intervention (Ali *et al.*, 1997) represents a system seeking to reduce behaviour problems and pupil exclusions from school and to lower the number of statements for BESD. As a guidance document, it was written as part of a Birmingham Education Department project between 1996 and 1997. It offers guidance for all schools and support services for all behaviour problems irrespective of whether they are seen as BESD, disciplinary or psychiatric, and involves a system rather than methods for changing the behaviour of children.

One of the core principles of the system was that 'problems with behaviour in education settings are usually a product of a complex interaction between the individual, school, family, community and wider society' (Daniels and Williams, 2000, p. 222). In its guidance on individual behaviour problems, the document proposes a series of three levels of intervention in which, particularly at level 1, systems perspectives are used.

Level 1, the initial referral part of the process, does not propose individual education programmes but rather is based on addressing the environment in which the behaviour arises and may relate to an individual pupil or groups of pupils. The process involves using a behavioural 'audit' aiming to achieve an optimal educational environment, that is, one that would exist, 'if every environmental improvement that it is reasonable to expect were made' (p. 222). The 'trigger' for level 1 is an expression of concern by any member of staff about any perceived behaviour problem. Importantly, the person expressing the concern normally keeps responsibility and power over the process through level 1 and is considered the lead person at this level.

In the approach, it is recommended that each school identify a behaviour co-ordinator (or in large schools, including secondary schools, a team) to whom the concerned member of staff takes the matter. The behaviour co-ordinator can give advice and help, in level 1, in carrying out the audit and producing a BEP. The lead person (usually the class or subject teacher) will normally carry out the audit by completing a behaviour environment checklist. This is a list of items covering factors affecting the environment (for example, the environment of the classroom or the playground) such as whole school policies, physical factors, classroom organisation and the personal style of the teacher. For example, in the Birmingham checklist, items on classroom management include 'a pupil's good behaviour is "named" and reflected back' and 'adult support is used to best effect' (p. 223).

Once the checklist is completed, the lead teacher may decide to tackle a certain area through the BEP. This is acceptable so long as it is practicable and has a connection to the behaviour causing concern. Before implementing the BEP, a baseline measure of the behaviour(s) causing concern is made so that the effectiveness of the plan is judged through its effects on the individual as well as the environment. The plan runs for at least six weeks. Behaviour problems arising during this time continue to be addressed under the school's normal procedures. The behaviour co-ordinator may also receive support from the educational psychologist or the behaviour support service teachers with a view to empowering the co-ordinator and the teacher who raised the matter. At the end of the life of the BEP, a review is held usually between the behaviour co-ordinator and the teacher (not the parent).

A move to level 2 of the Framework arises if the concern about the target behaviours continues even after the BEP has been implemented. At level 2, IBPs are introduced while the BEP continues to be implemented. The IBP, a form of IEP, involves the co-ordinator and the teacher working together, and the behaviour co-ordinator may be the lead person. The IBP may involve particular interventions such as counselling or individual reward systems.

Level 3 of the Framework centres on the IBP and may involve the work of people outside the school such as educational psychologists either to advise or to intervene directly.

After level 3, for pupils whose behaviour problems are severe but where it is judged they are not predominantly a special educational need, a joint action plan may be agreed between appropriate services to encourage joint working. Another option where it appears that there are SEN is statutory assessment.

Group work and circle time

Group work

Group work is an intervention that can be underpinned by different perspectives including cognitive-behavioural, psychodynamic and behavioural. Considering group work within the context of a systems approach is not intended to suggest that other perspectives are secondary in importance. However, there are features of some approaches to group work that share features of systems perspectives. For example, group considerations of problems and group solutions tend not to assume an individual locus for the problem, but see it as an aspect of the interaction between individuals and the contexts in which they function. The potential benefits of group work, so long as it is well planned and used appropriately, have been summarised as follows (Ayers and Prytys, 2002). It:

◆ provides opportunities for growth and development through sharing problems and experiences and for practising newly acquired skills and behaviours;
◆ enables children to learn new social skills and to increase their self-esteem;
◆ enables a larger number of children to be helped and is likely to be economic in time and cost.

(p. 116)

Some general points need to be borne in mind in preparing for group work with pupils considered to have BESD. The level of skills and training of the group leader(s) is important, including counselling skills, and the ability to be an effective facilitator. If a teacher is facilitating, the role of facilitating may need to be explained to and agreed with pupils participating in the group, and arrangements for supervising and supporting the group leaders themselves will require consideration. The behaviour of particular members can pose particular challenges in facilitating a group. Although group approaches tend to view problems in terms of interactions of the individual and the context, certain behaviour makes group interventions difficult. For example, group work may not suit pupils who may have very limited self-control or tend to be physically aggressive or destructive. (A lead into group work for such pupils can be facilitated by work with pairs of pupils.)

Furthermore, the group leader will need strategies for dealing with some of the behaviours that may emerge in the group such as disruption, monopolising and resistance. Parental/carer consent should be sought and the informed consent of the pupil established. A suitable room will be needed and consideration given to the length of the sessions (perhaps between an hour and two hours depending on such factors as the age of the children) and the number of sessions (possibly ten to encourage a focus on outcomes). (See also Geldard and Geldard, 2001.)

One example of group work in schools is that used as part of the Coping in Schools programme (McSherry, 2001, pp. 34–44). 'Reintegration groups' were developed in special schools for pupils with BESD and in pupil referral units for pupils assessed as being ready to prepare for transfer to mainstream school (p. 23). Group work has been used in primary schools to support pupils considered to be at risk of not coping with transfer to secondary school. The group work in that instance used the group as the basis for work on social skills, and on coping techniques to develop skills, 'through interaction with peers and adults in a supportive environment' (p. 34). The aim was to, 'help pupils to reflect on their skills in tackling difficult situations and promote the use of peer support to develop effective strategies' (p. 34).

Generally, the functions of the groups were to:

- raise self-esteem;
- foster a positive self-image;
- help to develop strategies;
- enable pupils to set their own targets;
- enable pupils to assess their own progress;
- develop the support and help of others in the group;
- offer positive reinforcement for pupils' successes.

(p. 36)

The groups normally comprised four to six young people facilitated by a supportive adult such as a teacher or learning mentor and they met in the same place and at the same time once a week. Confidentiality was agreed within the group.

Circle time

Circle time is an approach involving peer group work concentrating on sharing perceptions and dealing with any problems as a group. It typically involves teacher and pupils sitting in a circle for discussions and is carried out according to previously agreed guidelines. These include, for example, turn-taking and listening. Initially, the strategies and issues may be chosen by the teacher to help pupils eventually to focus on concerns and difficulties reflecting school and family issues. Children explore their feelings and concerns and consider solutions to difficulties. Trust, sharing and group responsibilities are central to the approach, which aims to develop self-esteem and confidence.

Circle time is used in an increasing number of schools and the example considered in this section is described as 'a systems approach to emotional and behavioural difficulties' (Kelly, 1999). It describes a collaborative project at a primary school in Scotland where a significant number of pupils were considered to have BESD and where this was considered to relate to pupils' low self-concept. This involved the introduction of circle time in both a whole-class setting and for groups taken out of class and appeared to lead to positive changes in behaviour of the targeted pupils, especially for whole-class interventions.

Initially, the head teacher of the school and the educational psychologist discussed with staff of the school the prospect of using a group approach and, following this, two teachers were invited to help plan and develop the project. These were the learning support teacher and a class teacher. A small planning group was formed which focused on the link between self-esteem and behaviour and a particular model of circle time (Mosley, 1996) was chosen as the method of group intervention. This was considered to be likely to improve self-concept and behaviour:

- ◆ [it] encourages positive feedback from child to child and teachers to child;
- ◆ it encourages positive self-statement;
- ◆ it ensures positive teacher attention and allows exploration of school-wide issues where difficulty is likely to occur . . .;
- ◆ it can be extended to become a whole school strategy;
- ◆ it promotes self-awareness and enhances open communication.

(Kelly, 1999, p. 41)

Circle of Friends

For pupils with BESD, who are perhaps withdrawn and vulnerable, setting up a Circle of Friends (Newton and Wilson, 1999) can help form links between the pupil and others. For example, in an ordinary school a pupil with BESD may spend part of the day with other pupils who have BESD and part of the day being taught with pupils in the rest of the school. A Circle of Friends can help ensure that, when the pupil with BESD is in the mainstream classroom and in the playground, there is a better opportunity to form good relationships with other pupils (e.g. Essex LEA, 1999; see also address list).

The teacher starting a Circle of Friends is often supported initially by someone, perhaps from outside the school and having previous experience of initiating such groups. If the approach is used with a class group, a person who does not usually teach the class will hold a preliminary discussion with the pupils. The child to be supported is not usually present but the approach will have been discussed with him and he will have given his agreement. The facilitator elicits from the pupils in the class descriptions of situations involving the focus child in which things go well and situations in which they do not. The pupils then consider their feelings when they have felt left out or lacking friends. The facilitator asks for ideas to improve the situation, and these might be suggestions such as sitting next to the focus child in a lesson or talking to him in the playground. The facilitator then asks for volunteers to form a Circle of Friends.

Later, school staff decide which volunteers will be chosen, selecting perhaps six children. The 'circle' then meets with the focus child and tells him all the positive things that were said and discusses how the focus child would like to be included in what they do. The circle meets periodically (perhaps weekly) to discuss how things are progressing and discuss what is working and what is not. This type of formal support might continue for a term or longer (see also Taylor, 1997).

Specialist intervention

Specialist intervention may be considered, such as the involvement of a person outside the school and the family systems. This person might be trained to fulfil a consultancy role or may be a family therapist. Such a specialist, in taking a systems view of the situation, would regard him- or herself as external to the systems of the family and the school. He or she would seek to bring to bear understandings from family therapy training and other theoretical backgrounds to help those involved develop an understanding of the context of the perceived problem.

Strengths of the systems approach and of specialist outside involvement are that they can help avoid or reduce the potential negative effects of labelling a child as being the sole or main cause of the problem. This can sidestep the use of (or at least lead to care when using) terms such as 'difficulty', which tend to locate the problem within the child.

However, bearing potentially negative or restrictive language in mind, some specialist therapeutic workers may hold perspectives that from a school's point of view may risk unnecessarily 'medicalising' the situation through the use of their terminology. They may be based at a 'clinic' and be trained as 'therapists'. Descriptions of work, for example one involving a child perceiving that he had to stand up for himself when it may have been inappropriate, are described as 'clinical examples' (Dowling and Osborne, 1994, p. 64).

School–family liaison

Where there is a school–family liaison worker, he or she may work independently or may be employed by the school or the LEA or others. Each of these employment and accountability alternatives can affect the way that families and the school view the worker. A school–family liaison worker may not necessarily be trained in consultancy or family therapy, but may work more pragmatically using the principle that it is generally better where there is a perceived problem that the school and the child's family communicate and that each tries to understand the views of the other where these differ. Such an approach may well accept the perspective of joint systems, even if it does not always explicitly and coherently draw on related approaches to intervention.

THINKING POINTS

Readers may wish to consider:

◆ the suitability of LEA-wide approaches drawing on systems perspectives;
◆ the applicability of class and group interventions, such as circle time;
◆ the potential usefulness of 'external' specialists, such as people trained in family therapy or in consultancy, to develop understanding and appropriate intervention concerning the joint systems of the school and the family;
◆ the extent to which insights and interventions relating to systems approaches can be effectively used by teachers and others working in schools.

KEY TEXTS

Dowling, E. and Osborne, E. (eds) (1994) *The Family and the School: A Joint Systems Approach to Problems with Children* (2nd edn), London, Routledge.

The first edition of this book was an early contribution to relating systems theory to both home and school and the second edition continues this theme.

Mosely, J. and Tew, M. (1999) *Quality Circle Time in the Secondary School: A Handbook of Good Practice*, London, David Fulton Publishers.

This, as the title indicates, offers guidance on what constitutes good practice in circle time provision for older pupils.

Chapter 3

Cognitive approach

INTRODUCTION

In this chapter, I seek to provide a rationale for a cognitive approach to interventions with pupils having BESD and explain how identification and assessment is viewed from this perspective while outlining some associated interventions. The interventions explained are cognitive aspects of emotional literacy, raising self-esteem through cognitive approaches, anxiety management and self-talk, and realigning the attribution of others. I also consider several approaches usually seen under the cognitive-behavioural umbrella: rational-emotive behavioural therapy (REBT); cognitive therapy; problem-solving approaches; and attribution theory and reattribution training. Aspects of such approaches are seen in anger management training, which the chapter also considers.

Rationale

This section defines cognition and explains how it may be used to account for certain BESD, and how this can lead to possible ways of reducing BESD. Cognition is a broad concept that relates to how one perceives and interprets events. This involves:

◆ thinking, planning and solving day-to-day problems;
◆ attributing apparent causes to events (perhaps taking a view that a certain event was a particular person's fault or responsibility);
◆ the development of self-perception and self-esteem;
◆ the formation and manifestation of various attitudes.

Cognitive approaches place particular emphasis on 'internal' phenomena, such as perception and memory, which one develops from experience and which influence one's current behaviour. Personal awareness of the environment and the ability to respond flexibly to it are considered important as are intuition and insight. The child is seen as an active participant in her learning – spontaneously activated to explore and learn.

In a cognitive approach to pupils with BESD, such processes are given careful consideration as a possible explanation for the difficulties, and as ways of dealing with them. For example, if a child or young person constantly thinks of himself as under threat from circumstances that others may cope with routinely, he is likely to become anxious. Should it prove possible to help the pupil deal with this anxiety, this might help him face 'threatening' situations and cope adequately, building confidence that might in turn reduce the anxiety. In short, if BESD are related to the way a child has come to perceive and interpret events, then being enabled to do so differently might lead to a reduction in the BESD.

Negative thought patterns might have been initially related to events when the child was really threatened but have continued and become ingrained so that they persist even when no real threat exists. More general negative perceptions of day-to-day occurrences (such as interactions at school) might similarly have been related to specific genuinely unpleasant events or unkindness, but again these may have become inappropriately entrenched as ways of perceiving and responding to school. Such perceptions and interpretations may be encouraged and amplified if other pupils, for example in a close-knit peer group, view school in a similar way. When such negative perceptions lead to antisocial and anti-school behaviour, the teaching staff and other pupils are likely to respond negatively, giving further 'reason' to continue the original negative behaviour so creating a vicious spiral.

Such, briefly, is the cognitive explanation of the origins and maintenance of BESD. The explanation also points the way towards how BESD might be identified and assessed and what the educational response to these difficulties might be.

Identification and assessment in the cognitive approach

It will be apparent that identification and assessment in this perspective depends on trying to establish the pupil's thinking processes such as his self-concept and his attributions (the way of attributing apparent causes to events perhaps being that a certain event was a particular person's fault). Self-concept influences self-esteem, which in turn is related to feelings of self-worth and can be assessed in various ways, for example by using assessments completed by the pupil or by the pupil and an adult working together (e.g. Morris, 2002, pp. 19–22).

The characteristic attributions of the pupil can be approached through questionnaires or through interviewing the pupil and discussing his perceptions and interpretations in detail. If, based on this, it appears that a satisfactory understanding of the BESD can be reached through the cognitive approach, then interventions may be considered. Both the assessment and interpretation of the pupil's cognition and the purpose and worthwhile nature of interventions will normally require that the pupil at some level accepts the interpretations of his difficulties as being credible. This suggests a level of openness and trust between the pupil and the person facilitating assessment and intervention that may be initially difficult and slow to establish.

Interventions drawing on a cognitive approach

Interventions often depend on trying to help the pupil perceive and interpret events and circumstances differently than he customarily does. The first four examples below relate to:

◆ cognitive aspects of emotional literacy involving setting the whole school context by encouraging pupils to develop the language of feelings;
◆ raising self-esteem;
◆ anxiety management and self-talk;
◆ working with others to recognise any changes in the child with BESD.

To the extent that these relate to behaviour, emotional states and social inter-action, changes in cognition are expected to lead to improvements in coping.

Cognitive aspects of emotional literacy

Emotional intelligence and emotional literacy

Emotional intelligence has been described in terms of the awareness and deploy-ment of feelings: being aware of one's feelings, managing them appropriately, 'marshalling' feelings so as to achieve one's goals, and 'recognising the feelings of others'. It is considered to include, 'self-motivation, self-control, persistence, delaying self-gratification, empathy and developing positive relationships with others and social competence' (Ayers and Prytys, 2002, p. 98). The parallel is of course with cognitive intelligence. The implication is that so-called emotional intelligence, like cognitive intelligence, is both important and represented by a range of skills and abilities.

Emotional literacy is a related notion. The analogy with literacy is perhaps an indication that emotional literacy can be taught, and fluency can be achieved in a similar way that literacy, in the usually accepted sense of reading, writing and spelling, can be taught. Emotional literacy has been defined as 'the practice of thinking individually and collectively about how emotions shape our actions and of using emotional understanding to enrich our thinking' (Antidote, 2003, p. v).

Emotional literacy and the school

Antidote, an organisation seeking to promote emotional literacy, has set out its own understanding of the approach, which I summarise below. Antidote expresses the view that, while emotional literacy may complement intensive work with 'trou-bled children', it should not replace it (p. 8). Emotional literacy may be seen as having five elements:

◆ developing the language of feelings;
◆ reflecting on feelings;
◆ taking an interest in what others are feeling;
◆ engaging in a dialogue about thoughts and feelings; and
◆ evolving a personal narrative.

(pp. 33–56)

The first three elements feed into 'engaging in a dialogue about thoughts and feelings'. This in turn contributes to 'evolving a personal narrative', which involves a person making out of all they have learned about themselves a narrative that 'enables them to experience their life as meaningful and valuable' (p. 33).

While emotional literacy is seen as involving the whole school community, certain contexts may contribute to it, including:

- circle time (and whole school 'well-being' meetings, peer mentoring and group discussions);
- peer support (including peer mentoring);
- Philosophy for Children (P4C) (including thinking skills and collaboration);
- therapeutic work (such as the role-play of 'real' incidents); and
- teaching the curriculum through dialogue (including teaching learning strategies and co-operative learning).

(pp. 58–82)

The qualities of an emotionally literate school are considered to relate to its working to realise six 'core values', namely: safety (emotional security), openness, compassion, connection, reflection and growth orientation (pp. 83–4).

Cognitive approaches in relation to emotional literacy

It will be seen that any attempt to develop a comprehensive view of emotional literacy draws on various approaches. Circle time can be related to systems approaches (and is considered in this book as an example of these). Depending on the particular orientation, drama and role-play may draw on psychotherapeutic perspectives. A cognitive view also informs several aspects of approaches that are considered to be part of emotional literacy. Among the most important of these cognitive elements is the development of a language for emotions. One assumption involved in this is that, in helping a child or young person develop a language for feelings, he will be able to express the emotions in words more effectively and communicate more directly. Others will then be made more aware and the child can be engaged in a dialogue about the feelings and how they might be understood.

One resource to encourage such language is *Zippy's Friends*, published by Partnership for Children (see address list). This is a programme for young children (it was developed for 6-year-olds), which involves a series of stories about Zippy, a stick insect, and his friends, a group of children. The stories involve them meeting issues such as friendship, bullying, feeling lonely, coping with loss and so on. The aim is to encourage children to talk about their feelings, to consider ways of dealing with them and to know where to go to get help.

Other approaches to encourage the use of the language of feelings, which can be employed in different ways with younger and older pupils, are puppets, role-play, drama and talking about imaginary situations ('What would you do if?'). The common theme of such methods is that they initially allow the pupil to talk about feelings in relation to imaginary things, which are distanced from the real concerns the pupil may have. However, they can and do provide opportunities for pupils to move on to talk about their own feelings and experiences more directly.

It is against such a background of whole-school opportunities for pupils to develop the language of feelings, and other opportunities for enhancing an understanding of emotions, that other interventions perhaps more specifically for pupils with BESD can be developed.

Raising self-esteem through cognitive approaches

Identity and self-esteem

Ideas and theories about the development of self-concept do not just come from cognitive theories. For example, in aspects of Sigmund Freud's theories (e.g. Freud, 2003 [1940]), it is suggested that the child begins to separate from the parent as the ego starts to develop and begins to form a sense of self. However, from a more cognitive viewpoint, as the child interacts with others, their reactions and the child's responses to those reactions contribute to the sense of who the child is. Where these 'others' are people with whom the child has regular and significant contact, the effect of their perceptions on the child are particularly influential.

As a child matures, he comes into contact with a wider circle of people who could influence him and he may filter or reject information that does not correspond with the emerging notion of the self. The people who influence the child's sense of self also change over time, either by force of circumstance, or through people choosing with whom they associate. Related to all this is the degree in which the child values or does not value himself.

A range of evidence supports the links between self-esteem and academic achievement (e.g. Lawrence, 1996). Self-esteem relates to feelings of self-value and self-worth and has been defined as depending on: self-knowledge, the extent to which one feels accepted, and on one's belief that one can influence other people and the environment (e.g. Morris, 2002, p. 3). Self-esteem, then, relates to knowledge, feelings and beliefs and it follows that among ways of raising the self-esteem of a child are approaches that draw on a cognitive perspective.

Assessments of self-esteem include a checklist known as *B/G Steem* (Maines and Robinson, 1988). This comprises a list of questions such as 'Do you worry a lot?' and 'Are other children unkind to you?', to which the pupil responds by circling a 'yes' or 'no' answer. It is intended to provide an indication of self-esteem and locus of control. As already indicated, the degree to which a person feels able to exert influence on their environment is an important aspect of self-esteem.

Interventions to encourage self-knowledge

Developing self-knowledge implies having a language to talk about feelings and attitudes, aspirations and beliefs and having opportunities to express and explore these. Teaching and counselling that encourage the pupil to develop a clearer sense of his feelings, behaviour and attitudes can help pupils with BESD, although it is an area that pupils may find difficult initially. This may be because the feelings are painful and disturbing. Or the child could put up a barrier against such communications because peer perceptions may suggest that they are signs of weakness.

Interventions intended to create more positive self-attributions

Through teaching and counselling, the pupil may come to consider ways in which attributes that the pupil views disparagingly might be genuinely and truthfully seen in a more positive light. Seeing oneself as 'boring' might be reaffirmed as having keen interests. Regarding oneself as 'slow' might be reinterpreted as being careful and thorough. Such reattributions do not occur overnight, particularly when young people may have had years of thinking about themselves in a negative way. They emerge and evolve slowly within trusting relationships in which an important other person (for example a teacher or counsellor) genuinely sees the young person in the more positive way. That important other person should be able to discuss this perspective with the child and present it as a genuine alternative way of viewing himself and the situations in which he finds himself.

At a more day-to-day level, the teacher and learning support assistant can ensure they frame their comments towards, and requests of, a child in more direct, positive terms rather than consistently negative ones. So, at the most basic level, 'You are not listening to me' becomes 'Listen to me' and 'Don't talk all the time' becomes 'Do your work'. An extra advantage of this approach is that it avoids the weakness of negative comments that they sometimes simply criticise but fail to make clear what the child should do to comply ('Don't talk all the time'). By contrast positive comments and requests indicate what the child should do ('Do your work').

Occasionally, even experienced teachers, especially when under stress, are not always aware of the extent to which negative comments can become ingrained in lessons and sometimes directed towards a very few pupils. When members of the senior management team or other colleagues in a school are observing lessons as part of subject or other monitoring, the teacher's effective use of positive and negative comments can be an aspect of the lesson that is constructively fed back to the teacher. Making a note of a selection of negative comments and discussing alternative phrasing that makes it clear what is expected of the pupil can be useful.

Anxiety management and self-talk

Should a pupil be anxious in certain situations, and should this be unrelated to any apparent 'real' cause for anxiety, he may be taught to first recognise the onset of the anxiety. This may involve being trained to be aware of increases in heart rate or recognising explicitly other signs, such as sweating palms. On recognising these signs, the pupil is taught to intervene himself through using an internal monologue, or 'self-talk'. This self-talk may be agreed and scripted so that the pupil knows it well. It is likely to involve elements that:

◆ encourage calmness;
◆ challenge the negative interpretation of the event or circumstances;

◆ seek to replace the negative interpretation with a credible and likely alternative interpretation.

Faced with a teacher that the pupil thinks dislikes him, the pupil may have a script such as:

> I will stay calm. The teacher has just asked me if I understand the question and I think she is are being sarcastic. But she might just be checking that I understand so that they can explain better. I will say that I don't understand and ask if the teacher would explain it again.

One explanation of such approaches is an assumption that thoughts and words influence each other. Negative thought patterns are considered to be set up by continually repeated, internal negative scripts. The person making a concerted effort to replace the negative scripts with positive ones can counteract these thought patterns. If thoughts lead to scripts that influence perceptions and behaviour, then relearned words, over a long period of time, can affect perceptions and responses.

Realigning the attributions of others

Another important intervention involves others rather than the pupil with BESD. It was pointed out earlier that the originally faulty attributions of the pupil considered to have BESD can be affirmed by the reactions of others to their negativity, so that there are real negative or hostile feelings directed towards him. If over a period of time the pupil with BESD manages to perceive and interpret differently, then it is important that others in his circle, including peers and teachers, do not still maintain their own negative attitudes and responses. These may of course be very subtle. Some work with others supporting the pupil's development and reinterpreting is likely to be necessary for any changes in the pupil to be long-lasting.

One vehicle for this can be the 'Circle of Friends' approach (e.g. Newton and Wilson, 1999) already discussed in Chapter 2. This encourages peers to provide support to a pupil and engage in joint problem-solving with him. Initially, an educational psychologist or another suitable person from outside the school talks with the whole class without the pupil present but with the permission of parents and pupil. As a result, a small group of children are enlisted who agree to meet regularly with the child. The teacher or a counsellor meets with the group to act as a facilitator and to help the group identify problems and strategies. In the particular context of developing a group around the child, who are sensitive to his changed and changing attributions, the role of the group and the particular problems that they tackle will be informed by this.

A cognitive-behavioural perspective

A cognitive-behavioural perspective can be in part explained with reference to cognitive-behavioural therapies. Such therapies, it has been suggested, 'represent hybrids of behavioural strategies and cognitive processes, with the goal of achieving behavioural and cognitive change' (Dobson and Dozois, 2001, pp. 11–12).

From the cognitive-behavioural viewpoint, behaviour is seen as influenced by cognition (attitudes and assumptions) and by cognitive appraisal (the processes of thinking and reasoning). Interventions involve monitoring the cognitions; seeking connections between thoughts, feelings and behaviour; and seeking to replace negative cognitions with positive ones. The particular interventions considered below are REBT; cognitive therapy; problem-solving approaches; and attribution theory and reattribution training. Aspects of these approaches are evident in anger management training from a cognitive perspective, which is also considered.

Rational-emotive behavioural therapy

REBT was originated by Albert Ellis (see, e.g., Ellis *et al.*, 1997) and centrally concerns rational and irrational beliefs. It views BESD as predominantly self-created and arising from beliefs, interpretations and evaluations of what happens in a person's life. Beliefs are held about oneself, others and about one's environment and these beliefs can influence thought, emotions and behaviour. The beliefs, whether positive or negative in their effect, can be modified. Rational beliefs are self-enhancing and the consequences of rational beliefs are healthy negative emotions such as sorrow or concern.

But irrational beliefs are self-defeating and contribute towards BESD. Irrational thinking is characterised by absolutist thoughts and by inferences that cannot be substantiated. Such thinking can lead to unhealthy negative emotions such as anger, anxiety and guilt. Psychological problems are considered to be brought about by ego disturbance – absolutist demands directed at oneself; or by 'discomfort disturbance' – absolutist demands concerning conditions.

A cognitive ABC analysis can be used in this context in which 'A' is an *activating event* such as perceptions and inferences; 'B' is rational and irrational *beliefs*; and 'C' is the emotional and behavioural *consequences*.

Adaptive behaviour is encouraged by putting right irrational thinking or by modifying it. It is believed that it is mainly current beliefs that disturb people rather than the past, which is what is meant when this approach considers BESD to be self-created. Change takes place when the child or young person works on their irrational beliefs through dialogue with a therapist. The beliefs are identified, discussed and challenged and are tested empirically, logically and pragmatically.

Cognitive therapy

Cognitive therapy developed from the work of Aaron Beck (e.g. Beck *et al.*, 1979) and concerns the cognitive processes of perceiving, thinking and reasoning and their effect on behaviour and emotions. A person constructs their own beliefs and experiences and beliefs can be sampled through such methods as self-reports. Important concepts are automatic thoughts; cognitive schema; and cognitive deficits and distortions.

Automatic thoughts, unlike voluntary thoughts, seem to arise spontaneously, are hard to control and may cause distress. Cognitive schemas, formed by early learning experiences, are deep cognitive processes that determine a person's view of the world, himself and his relationships with others. Once activated, cognitive schemas are maintained and reinforced by cognitive distortions (such as over-generalising), which bias the selection of information to support the existing schemas. Cognitive deficits for example in memory or perception (such as being unable to sufficiently recognise the consequences of one's actions) also help maintain schemas. As a result of these processes, thinking and reasoning become inflexible and judgements become absolute (typified by language or perceptions such as 'must' and 'ought').

BESD arise as exaggerations of normal responses. Intervention involves a therapist encouraging the child or young person to reappraise beliefs logically and empirically. This includes looking for different explanations of events, different ways of acting and responding and different ways of behaving. In turn, this depends on the active involvement and motivation of the child or young person.

Problem-solving approaches

In this perspective, a child with BESD is considered to lack, or to have to only a very limited degree, the problem-solving skills that are necessary for effective social functioning. Problem-solving approaches have cognitive and behavioural elements and use structured programmes to help a child with BESD to approach his problems.

For example, problem-solving skills training (D'Zurilla, 1986) involves being aware of the problem; defining and formulating the problem; putting forward alternative solutions; deciding the approach; and testing the solution. Participants are trained to identify problems, prevent their initial impulses, come up with various alternatives, think about the possible consequences, plan their solutions and evaluate them.

More generally, in interactions with children, teachers and learning support assistants can use problem-solving dialogues to help pupils analyse situations and deal with them better. For example, Glenys Fox, writing for assistants working in schools, suggests strategies and questions to help problem-solving that include:

- talking with the pupil about sharing the problem;
- looking for times when the problem is not there;
- considering whether changes in what appeared to lead to the problem might be useful; and
- looking at whether and how the pupil successfully dealt with similar problems in the past.

(Fox, 2001, pp. 69–70)

Attribution theory and reattribution training

The importance of a pupil's attributions and the sensitivity of others to changes in these have already been touched on. Attribution theory is a broad term for several approaches, many with a cognitive slant, that seek to analyse the way in which people use information to explain why they and others behave in the way they do. These are referred to as causal attributions. Among the biases in the attribution process are the 'actor observer effect', the 'hostile attribution bias' and the 'false consensus effect'. In the actor observer effect, people attribute their own behaviour to the circumstances and the behaviour of others to the others' disposition. The hostile attribution bias involves people tending to interpret ambiguous behaviours as being an indication of hostile attitudes or intentions. In the false consensus effect, people view their own behaviour as normal and consider that others would behave in a similar way in a similar situation. Consequently the person believes that others should behave in the same way that he does. People vary in the way they make attributions, examples being to do with locus of control and with attributional style. People having an internal locus of control consider that they have control over reinforcing events. Those with an external locus of control believe that reinforcing events are outside their control, within the remit of luck, or under the control of other people. Attributional style is determined according to a person's tendency to make certain kinds of attributions rather than others.

From the perspective of attribution theory, BESD are regarded as following on from a person's tendency to make unproductive or negative attributions about their feelings and behaviours and those of others. For example, a child with a hostile attribution bias may interpret a teacher's behaviour that is ambiguous as being hostile in attitude or intent. The child's own behaviour in response may therefore be confrontational. In the false consensus effect, the pupil may view his own unacceptable behaviour as normal, believing that others would behave in a similar way in a similar situation, and that others should behave in the way that he does. Therefore attempts to modify the pupil's behaviour will be made all the more difficult.

An approach considered suitable in such circumstances is reattribution training. This is an attempt to train the child or young person to make more positive causal attributions and more accurate attributions about their own behaviour and that of others.

Anger management training

Anger, perhaps arising when a child feels threatened, thwarted or mistreated and expressed verbally and physically, and sometimes followed by aggressive outbursts, may be seen as a way of expressing what it is that is making the child angry. From a cognitive point of view, anger is understood in relation to such factors as the child's expectations, how he interprets events and how he reacts to them.

Cognitive appraisal is important. A person, situation or event may be perceived as hostile when most people would regard it as neutral or ambiguous. Such distortions of appraisal can precipitate inappropriate anger. An initial assessment can use a cognitive ABC analysis, where the reader will remember that 'A' stands for the 'activating event', 'B' represents the child's 'beliefs' and 'C' is the 'consequences'. More specifically, the 'activating event' is the child's perception of the events leading up to anger and the inferences that he makes about these events. The child's 'beliefs' will be either rational or irrational convictions about the events or people that activated the anger. 'Consequences', both emotional and behavioural, are what follows from maintaining rational and irrational beliefs with regard to the people and situation concerned.

Such an ABC analysis carried out in discussion with the pupil can lead to the child beginning to recognise the people and events that trigger anger and what he perceives in relation to them. Such perceptions and feelings become the focus of interventions and the development of anger management skills. These skills include:

◆ Self-reflection – 'Why do I feel anger in these situations or towards this person?' 'Is the anger helping the situation or making it worse?'
◆ Problem-solving – 'What are the different ways in which a situation in which I normally feel anger could be dealt with?'
◆ Taking alternative perspectives – 'Are there other ways in which the situation or the person could be legitimately viewed?' 'Might some of these other ways be more in line with what might "really" be happening?' 'What would be the consequences if I were able to view the situation in a different way?'

Drawing on such considerations, one approach is for the teacher, or other adult, to work with the pupil to develop self-instructions to rehearse and learn for use when faced with the situation or people that trigger anger. This will involve developing an internal monologue to remain calm, to listen carefully to what is being said, to reflect on what is being said, to look for positive alternative explanations, to consider various responses, to evaluate the responses and to respond accordingly. For such a complex process to become automatic and part of everyday life, a child who is not used to reflecting and responding in this way needs practice and support in applying the skills. The practice begins with the discussions that lead up to the sort of scripts that are deemed suitable. The pupil rehearses these verbally and in action using role-play. After the role-play, the pupil will be encouraged to talk about the self-instruction used. Where there is evidence that the pupil has made an attempt to use the approach in day-to-day situations, this is praised and encouraged. (See also Blum, 2001.)

THINKING POINTS

Readers may wish to consider:

◆ the pupils in a particular school who are identified as having BESD and decide whether, for any, a cognitive perspective provides a credible explanation and possible response to the pupil;
◆ whether interventions would be likely to be more effective if they involved (following training) staff who know the pupils well or whether outside support, for example, from an educational or clinical psychologist might be more effective.

KEY TEXTS

Antidote (2003) *The Emotional Literacy Handbook*, London, David Fulton Publishers.

This book draws together elements of various perspectives and advocates them as whole-school approaches to encourage individual and collective thought about how motions shape one's actions and how emotional understanding may be used to enrich thinking.

Dobson, K. S. (ed.) (2003) *Handbook of Cognitive-Behavoural Therapies* (2nd edn), London, Guilford Press.

Part one of the book deals with conceptual issues, while part two describes various therapies including 'Problem solving therapies' (Chapter 7), 'Rational emotive behaviour therapy' (Chapter 9) and 'Cognitive therapy' (Chapter 10). There is also a chapter on 'Cognitive-behavioural therapy with youth' (Chapter 7) which touches on several approaches including relaxation training, affective education and cognitive restructuring.

Chapter 4

Behavioural approach

INTRODUCTION

This chapter explains a rationale for behavioural approaches and touches on how the causes of BESD are viewed. I explain how BESD are identified and assessed with reference to a range of behaviours. The chapter explains some fundamentals of behavioural interventions: the context of the interventions; reinforcement including the differential reinforcement of other behaviour; generalisation; over-correction; time out; fading; imitation; desensitisation; and modelling (drawing on social learning theory). I examine some vehicles for behavioural intervention: contracts; token economy; social skills training; and a programme using an 'ante-cedent, behaviour, consequence' (ABC) approach to challenging behaviour.

Rationale

Many behavioural approaches derive from learning theory (e.g. Skinner, 1968) and cognitive mediational accounts of behavioural change (e.g. 1974; Bandura, 1969). Behaviour modification has been used with pupils having different SEN, including children with severe learning difficulties, as well as with pupils with BESD. It is used as an aspect of teaching techniques, for example in precision teaching where techniques such as chaining, shaping, fading and prompting may be used (e.g. Farrell, 2003, pp. 128–9). Behavioural therapy has been described as 'the application of the technique, methods, principles and assumptions of modern behaviour theory and science to human problems' (Hayes *et al.*, 1994, p. 132).

Behavioural approaches emphasise what is observable rather than what might (possibly erroneously) be assumed to be the pupils' thoughts, motivations and attitudes, although in modern behavioural approaches these are not ignored. A pupil with BESD is seen as having learned certain patterns of behaviour that are normally unacceptable or are considered unhealthy. He may have modelled his behaviour on a parent/carer or another adult or sibling whose behaviour was violent, unpredictable and excessively solitary, or in some other way dysfunctional.

Parents and others may have inadvertently rewarded his behaviour when it was unacceptable, for example by persistently giving in to tantrums. In these and other ways, the pupil has learnt the inappropriate behaviour. It follows from this that the behaviour can be unlearned or replaced by other behaviour that is more acceptable to other people. The various behavioural interventions seek to do this.

In reality and in practice, behaviour (including verbal behaviour) is not usually regarded in such an isolated way and it is accepted that there are thoughts and perceptions and other, loosely called, 'internal' factors that influence behaviour. Also, as far as is practicable, the pupil is involved in discussions about his behaviour, targets for behavioural change and the evaluation of approaches to encourage acceptable behaviour and discourage unwanted behaviour.

Causes of BESD

The behavioural approach sees BESD as being brought about in the same sort of way as other behaviours. The child may observe and copy unacceptable behaviour such as violence. He may be 'rewarded' for unacceptable behaviour such as temper tantrums by getting the attention of parents and others, who come to act as 'reinforcers'. In this approach, the supposed causes of the unwanted behaviour provide the rationale for changing them by setting up different ways of encouraging and discouraging various behaviours.

Identification and assessment relating to unwanted behaviour

The identification and assessment of BESD relates to a range of the child's behaviours. This may not always be obviously unacceptable behaviour towards others such as unwarranted aggressive behaviour or damage to property. It can also include withdrawn or fearful behaviour that does not explicitly interfere with others but that limits the child's opportunities to participate in education and school life.

Given that the eventual aim is to modify the pupil's behaviour, detailed observations of the behaviour that it is proposed to change are necessary. The observer has to specify clearly the conduct to be observed, for example making inappropriate noises in class, in purely behavioural terms. Sometimes the description of the behaviour will be refined as observations are made, so that further observations are necessary using the refined definitions. For example, it may be decided in observing a pupil making inappropriate noises in class that it is only those noises that are loud enough to disturb others that should be the focus of intervention.

Once the behaviour is specifically described, the teacher, psychologist or other person making the observations will record its frequency. The observer might note, for example, the number of times in a specified period that the behaviour occurs, say 20 times in a ten-minute period, so that this forms the baseline for subsequent intervention.

Another approach is to look at the duration of the behaviour rather than its frequency. This would be useful if the behaviour was discrete (having clear boundaries and usually brief) and not very frequent. Using a stopwatch, the observer times each occurrence of the behaviour. This makes it possible to compare samples of unequal duration by calculating the percentage of time spent on the behaviour under consideration.

Although it gives a measure of behaviour that is not as precise as some other methods, instantaneous time sampling is useful if the behaviour is very frequent or indiscrete. A time interval of say ten seconds is decided upon and, at the end of every time interval, the child is observed and a note made whether or not the specified behaviour is occurring. This allows the teacher to calculate the number of times the child is engaged in the specified behaviour as a percentage of the total number of time intervals observed.

Event sampling is used for behaviours that occur relatively infrequently. It allows the teacher or other observer to focus on the antecedents and consequences of the behaviour. Features of the child's environment are noted when the specified behaviour occurs. For example, if a child swearing is the specified behaviour to be modified, it may be found to occur if other children or another particular child is in close proximity (possible antecedents). The observer may find that anxious teacher attention or the approval of some pupils (possible consequences) follows the unwanted behaviour.

Such observations help refine and develop the teacher's understanding of the behaviour in question. The teacher considers the factors that appear to be influencing the behaviour. The child's behaviour may be observed in different settings and comparisons made. From all this, the teacher will develop a hypothesis about the behaviour. For example, if the teacher believes that a child is shrieking to avoid doing a task then she would expect that in a session of free play, when the child has a choice of activities, the behaviour would decrease. Such a hypothesis would be tested and either confirmed or disconfirmed.

Some fundamentals of behavioural intervention

The context of interventions

The context in which it is proposed that behavioural intervention be made is important. For example, the school and the classroom should operate with clear rules for behaviour. These should be as few as practicable and should be expressed as far as possible in terms of what pupils should do rather than what they should not. If the rules are discussed, negotiated and agreed with pupils, they are more likely to be understood and respected. For some pupils who find unstructured times such as morning and afternoon breaks and lunchtimes difficult, the opportunity for structured activities will help. Against such a background, the encouragement of acceptable behaviours and the discouragement of unwanted behaviours, which are staples of a behavioural approach, are more likely to make sense to pupils.

Reinforcement and programmes and schedules of reinforcement

Reinforcement is a key concept in behaviour modification although it is often misunderstood; in particular negative reinforcement is often incorrectly equated with punishment. Reinforcement has to do with the consequences of behaviour, which affect its frequency. Reinforcers may be primary (e.g. food) or secondary (e.g. praise, 'tokens' that can be traded in for rewards). Successful reinforcers to be at their most effective should be immediate, consistent and exclusively associated with the desired (or undesirable) behaviour.

A distinction is made between positive and negative reinforcement. Positive reinforcement, such as reward, tends to increase the frequency of the behaviour to which it is applied. This can be turned on its head so that one can say that something that tends to increase the frequency of a specified behaviour is acting as a reward. This indicates that one does not have to have a fixed idea of what a person is likely to find rewarding but that the reward can be defined according to its effect.

Negative reinforcement involves the removal of an unpleasant stimulus (e.g. repeated reminders of forgotten homework) when a desired behaviour occurs, the aim being that the learner should modify his behaviour to avoid the unpleasant stimulus. This relates to avoidance conditioning in which active avoidance involves the person performing a response to avoid an aversive stimulus while passive avoidance involves the person desisting from an action in order to avoid an aversive stimulus. The 'negative' aspect of this process refers not to the unpleasant stimulus but to the negating of it when the appropriate behaviour is performed or the inappropriate behaviour is stopped.

Punishment involves the linking of an unpleasant stimulus (e.g. detention) with unacceptable behaviour or the removal of a pleasurable activity, object or privilege (response cost). The punishment has the effect of reducing or eliminating the behaviour to which it is linked. Again one does not have to have in mind what is likely to act as a punishment and it can be defined as something that tends to reduce the undesirable behaviour. An example of the use of punishment is an adaptation of over-correction. When an undesirable behaviour such as damage to property or a physical assault occurs, a desirable behaviour is performed repeatedly as a punishment. Such an approach should be carefully planned and monitored. Among the disadvantages of punishment (e.g. Ayers and Prytys, 2002: 171) is that it may simply suppress the unwanted behaviour; that it is not always clear to the child what the appropriate behaviour should be; that it suggests that aggressive behaviour is acceptable; and that it can create dislike and avoidance.

Extinction involves eliminating the reinforcers of unacceptable behaviour. For example, tantrums may be reinforced by adult attention. Therefore, denying the adult attention while at the same time ensuring a child's safety would tend to reduce the incidence of tantrums. In practice, with pupils with BESD the use of reinforcers usually involves reinforcing acceptable or desired behaviour (positive reinforcement) and striving to avoid reinforcing behaviour that is not desired (extinction).

A programme that aims to reduce the rate of undesirable behaviour tends to be more effective when positive reinforcement is given for other acceptable behaviour. The differential reinforcement of *alternative* behaviour involves rewarding the learner for, as it were, not exhibiting the unwanted behaviour. The differential reinforcement of *incompatible* behaviour refers to rewarding behaviour that is incompatible with the undesired behaviour. For example, if the unwanted behaviour is throwing items across the classroom, then, clearly, rewarding quiet participation in a task is likely to increase the likelihood of behaviour that is incompatible with the unwanted behaviour. Informal applications of this principle are sometimes referred to as 'catching the pupil being good'.

Schedules of reinforcement refer to the number or type of responses that will be rewarded. Positive reinforcers are given according to a schedule. In continuous reinforcement, every occurrence of a particular behaviour is reinforced, a strategy suitable when desired behaviour is just emerging but one which is less successful in the longer term. Intermittent reinforcement involves rewarding the child for only some of the desired behaviours. This tends to prevent the child being saturated with rewards, makes the administration of rewards more manageable and tends to ensure that the desired behaviour continues for longer after the reinforcement ceases.

Generalisation

Generalisation occurs when a behaviour that has been learned in one situation happens spontaneously in another. For example, a child may have learned to stay in his seat for a specified period in his regular classroom when it is required as part of the lesson. Generalisation is considered to have occurred if the child who had previously been out of his seat inappropriately now remains in his seat when in another classroom.

Over-correction

An example of over-correction as a form of punishment was mentioned earlier. Other types include 'restitutional over-correction', in which the child removes or repairs any damage caused and 'positive practice over-correction', which involves the learner practising types of appropriate behaviour. Over-correction of any kind should be carefully planned and monitored.

Time out

As mentioned earlier, using reinforcers usually involves reinforcing acceptable or desired behaviour and striving to avoid reinforcing behaviour that is not desired. Time out can be used to avoid the child receiving positive reinforcement for unwanted behaviour. For example, the teacher might hypothesise that the attention of peers is positively reinforcing the unwanted behaviour of a pupil. If this hypothesis is correct, then temporarily removing that reinforcement immediately the unwanted behaviour occurs is likely to reduce the unwanted behaviour. The period of removal from the group is normally no longer than two or three minutes and the learner is allowed to join the group after showing, even if only briefly, the desired behaviour. If the period of time out is longer than a few minutes, the pupil is likely to forget why he is in the time out area and so the learning link between the inappropriate behaviour *not* leading to a reward is lost. Time out tends to work more effectively if the pupil is warned about what will happen and if the behaviour that leads to time out is pointed out and the purpose of time out explained.

Fading

In the technique of 'fading' a new stimulus or prompt is presented beside an existing stimulus to which a learned response already exists. The 'old' stimulus is then phased out (faded) and the new stimulus takes control over the learned response. A child may have learned to tidy away work (learned response) when reminded by the teacher (stimulus). I will call the teacher reminder the 'old' stimulus. If the teacher and the pupil wish the pupil to remember to tidy away work without the teacher's reminder, the pupil can be prompted to respond to a new stimulus, e.g. observing several other pupils who tidy away on time. (In fact in this case the potential stimulus will have been present before but it will not have acted as a stimulus for the pupil.) This will come to replace the teacher reminder as the stimulus to tidy away work on time. The new stimulus (that of other pupils tidying away) is presented/noticed beside the existing stimulus (teacher reminder) to which a learned response (tidying away) already exists. The old stimulus (teacher reminder) is then faded and the new stimulus (other pupils tidying) takes control over the learned response.

Imitation

Imitation is a vehicle for learning new behaviour. More informally, of course, imitation is operating much of the time as the child sees the way others behave and copies it. It may be used explicitly in role-play when an adult demonstrates a desired behaviour such as expressing a preference appropriately (for example without swearing). The pupil's attempts at imitation may be encouraged by explicit positive reinforcement.

Desensitisation

Desensitisation may be used in behaviour therapy for managing fears such as school phobia. The object or situation that evokes the fear is introduced in manageable phases and a picture or a model of the school may be introduced first. Approaches such as associating the feared object or situation with a pleasurable experience such as soothing music are used to help the child control the fear. The real feared object or situation is gradually introduced. Obviously, in the case of something such as school phobia, the school will also work to ensure that any events that may have precipitated or sustained the fear, such as bullying, are also tackled.

Systematic desensitisation, a form of behaviour therapy developed by Joseph Wolpe, involves the person imagining increasingly greater anxiety-producing situations while at the same time engaging in behaviour that reduces the anxiety, such as deep relaxation. The first step is to learn the behaviour that reduces the anxiety (e.g. relaxation). The child then orders the situations that cause anxiety in a hierarchy. Finally, he imagines the situations while engaged in the anxiety-reducing behaviour. For older children, the approach can be helpful in dealing with anxiety and phobias.

Modelling

Modelling is an intervention associated with social learning theory, a theory having elements of both behavioural and cognitive approaches. Associated with the work of Bandura (1977) and Mischel (1968), the approach emphasises the notion that not only are people affected by their environment but that they affect the environment too. Cognition is important as people actively process the information they receive from their environment. A person's behaviour can be variable and the effect of surroundings is taken into account. An important aspect is a person's perceived ability to control his behaviour and what happens as a result of it. This self-efficacy can have an impact on a person's behaviour, feelings and motivation. Behaviours and different situations are taken into account when making judgements about a person's self-efficacy. Other central features are 'observational learning' and 'self-regulation'. Observational learning concerns behaviour learned by observing the behaviour of others. Self-regulation, controlling one's own behaviour, involves rewarding and punishing oneself in relation to self-imposed standards. It will be seen that behaviour is important in the social learning model because it is the behaviour of others that influences the way a child behaves because he tends to copy observed behaviour of people who are important to him. Also, the aim is to modify the child's behaviour by providing alternative models and by encouraging the child to copy that observed behaviour.

Against the background of social learning theory, modelling draws on the observational learning of behaviour. This involves attention, retention, reproduction and motivation. If children (and adults for that matter) learn by observing the behaviour of others, this can be structured if a child's behaviour is unacceptable, by guiding the behaviour that the child observes and copies. In special sessions, a teacher or learning support assistant might demonstrate (model) desired behaviour. The pupil would be encouraged to observe the behaviour closely (attention), remember it in the form of words or symbols (retention) and copy it (reproduction). The adult will guide and encourage this process because, in order to attend, remember and copy, the child has to be motivated. As well as behaviour being learned by modelling, emotional responses can be learned in this way too.

Vehicles for behavioural interventions

While the techniques relating to reinforcement, generalisation, over-correction, time out, fading, imitation, desensitisation and modelling are used to modify behaviour, some approaches draw on these and other techniques in a broader way. These vehicles include contracts, token economy, social skills training and programmes using an 'antecedent, behaviour, consequence' approach to challenging behaviour.

Contracts

Contracts agreed between the pupil (and parents) and the school can be an effective way of formalising a behavioural arrangement. The contract might specify the behaviour expected of the pupil and the rewards he will receive for it. It may set out the behaviour in which the pupil may not engage and the sanctions that will be imposed if such behaviour occurs.

An important part of any contract is the discussion and negotiation that takes place before the contract is agreed. The writing out of the contract, carefully reading over its conditions and agreeing to it perhaps by signing it are intended to set out clearly the requirements of the pupil's behaviour. It follows that, should any changes to the contract be thought to be required, these should be negotiated and agreed by all parties (Spiegler and Guivrement, 1998).

Token economy

A token economy is a form of developed behaviour modification that is used in some mainstream learning support units and some special schools for pupils with BESD. It is more difficult to implement in an everyday mainstream school setting because to work well it requires a level of consistency and predictability that is difficult to sustain.

Tokens are effectively secondary reinforcers, which pupils trade in for different rewards. The tokens may be points that are recorded or points accompanied by plastic disks that are given to the pupil. Care is taken that pupils know that the tokens are only valid if the teacher also records the points so that illicit trading in tokens is discouraged.

This allows the tokens to be given immediately the desired behaviour occurs, increasing the likelihood that the presentation of the token will reinforce the behaviour. It also enables a varied menu of rewards to be developed that motivate pupils and capture their attention. The reward menu is often developed in consultation with the pupils and can range from food treats, to a trip out, to a toy or to a valued item such as a compact disc.

A method of punishment called 'response cost' is sometimes used in token economy systems in which tokens are deducted when a specified undesirable behaviour occurs. Such an approach is carefully planned and monitored.

Token economies can engage the imagination of younger pupils. For example, in Chelfham Mill School, Devon, a special school for boys with BESD, themes chosen in discussion with pupils, and lasting for several months, are used for the token economy. The theme might be racing car driving where points are represented by the progress of cars, each one representing a particular child round a racetrack. These are visually presented in both the class-room and in the residential setting. The points in such a system of course still earn privileges but the visual representation engages pupils' imagination and motivation.

Social skills training

Social skills in the context being discussed are considered to be those patterns of behaviour that tend to indicate recognition of, and respect for, others and the skills associated with acceptable personal and social interactions. To the extent that a pupil with BESD lacks such skills or possesses them only to a limited extent, his capacity to engage in and develop positive personal and social contacts with a wide variety of people is impaired.

An important precursor to social skills training is therefore the identification of which skills appear to be lacking or are rudimentary given the pupil's age. To help assure the motivation of the pupil and his fullest co-operation in any subsequent intervention, such assessment needs to be performed with sensitivity and with the pupil's involvement. A pupil's self-reported level of proficiency in social skills can be a good starting point. If the pupil accurately considers himself to be lacking in some aspects of social skills, the teacher does not have to begin by suggesting these and persuading the pupil that they are lacking. The teacher can encourage the pupil to include in the self-report aspects of social and personal skills that are developed comparatively well so that the assessment is not exclusively negative and so that, as necessary, positive skills can be drawn on to develop rudimentary ones.

An interview with the pupil can yield similar information to that emerging from a self-report or can be used to supplement self-report information. A more structured format might include the use of a checklist or rating scale completed by the pupil and also perhaps a version completed by the teacher or others based on observation of the pupil's behaviour in different settings. The two or more assessments may be compared to help develop an idea of the sorts of skills on which the pupil might work.

Given such assessments, the next aspect of the procedure is for the teacher to seek to reach agreement with the pupil that certain social skills are lacking or underdeveloped and that it would be beneficial for the pupil to learn or further develop these skills. This leads to agreeing what repertoire of social skills will be taught. As Ayers and Prytys (2002) point out, for a pupil to be able to perform a social skill, he must, 'be able to know how and when to perform the skills, be competent at the skill and be motivated to perform the skill' (p. 198).

The initial motivation can be encouraged by sensitive identification and assessment of skills deficits as outlined earlier. But the subsequent motivation will be developed as and when the pupil sees positive effects in personal and social interactions or when the pupil has the desire to apply the skills. Knowing how to perform a skill and becoming competent in it can begin with training but application in real-life situations is also of course necessary. The application is also part of the knowledge of when to use the skills.

Among the skills that are taught are:

◆ conversational skills (active listening, turn-taking, eye contact and other aspects of non-verbal communication);
◆ appropriate ways of expressing emotions verbally;
◆ criticising in a way that avoids the person being criticised feeling demeaned;
◆ receiving criticism and responding suitably;
◆ negotiating successfully.

Among ways of training social skills are reinforcement, 'modelling' and demonstration. Other approaches include instruction, rehearsal/practice, role-play and feedback. Consider the example of seeking to develop the social skills of receiving (fair) criticism and responding in a way appropriate to the criticism and the context.

Having identified and assessed these in co-operation with the pupil as an area on which to work, the teacher can begin with discussion and instruction outlining and agreeing ways in which the pupil could suitably respond. These might include listening, reflecting, answering the criticism, apologising if this is justified and so on. The pupil could then observe the teacher or peers demonstrate some of the suitable responses or watch a video conveying the same. The pupil would then practise the skills perhaps in a role-play setting and discuss afterwards with the teacher how effective the skills were and how they might be further improved. As the pupil achieves some level of skill, a video recording of his skills can be made that the pupil can watch, both to see progress and to suggest how further improvements might be made.

Programmes using an 'ABC' approach to challenging behaviour

A so-called antecedent, behaviour, consequences approach ('ABC' approach) can be successful with pupils with challenging behaviour through adaptations of the basic principles of behaviour modification. Challenging behaviour can be analysed according to its antecedents, the behaviour itself and its consequences. Antecedents and consequences may be sustaining the challenging behaviour.

If a programme is devised to replace the unwanted behaviour with desired behaviour, the desired behaviour should have similar reinforcing consequences to the unwanted behaviour.

For example, the child may see food (antecedent), cause disruption (behaviour) and receive the food (consequence). New communicative behaviours can be taught to replace the unwanted behaviour, say, by teaching the child to use a non-verbal sign rather than disruption to convey his intention.

Other programmes may teach other functionally related behaviours to replace the unwanted behaviour. For example, a child in an environment that he finds over-stimulating (antecedent) may scream (behaviour) in order to be removed (consequence). Instead, the child may be taught to listen to peaceful music on a headset to suppress an over-stimulating environment instead of shrieking.

A programme may involve changing the events leading up to the inappropriate behaviour. The behaviour may indicate a wish to escape from a situation perhaps because it involves learning that the pupil finds too difficult (antecedent). If the tasks were simplified and errorless learning was introduced (antecedent removed), the inappropriate behaviour would be less likely to be sustained.

THINKING POINTS

Readers may wish to consider:

◆ the degree to which behavioural perspectives satisfactorily explain some of the BESD with which they are concerned;
◆ the extent to which their setting (LEA or school for example) provides a range of behavioural interventions;
◆ how the effectiveness of such interventions is monitored so that the approaches can be refined and improved.

KEY TEXT

Tilstone, C. and Layton, L. (2004) *Child Development and Teaching Pupils with Special Educational Needs*, London, Routledge.

In this book, Chapter 4, 'Skinner and the learning theorists', outlines the work of Thorndyke, Pavlov and Watson; Skinner; and Bandura's social learning theory. Chapter 7, also titled 'Skinner and the learning theorists' touches on educational applications such as prompting, shaping, modelling and chaining.

Chapter 5

Psychodynamic and related approaches

INTRODUCTION

In this chapter, I summarise a psychodynamic approach to BESD. The chapter looks at causal factors and at the identification and assessment of BESD in the psychodynamic approach. I describe various interventions. First, the chapter examines therapies that are mainly psychodynamic or draw on aspects of the approach. These are play therapy, music therapy, art therapy, drama therapy and movement therapy. I look at the contribution of nurture groups, which developed from the work of psychoanalyst John Bowlby.

I then move from a consideration of predominantly psychodynamic approaches to an examination of more eclectic ones with elements that are also evident in psychodynamic perspectives, namely a focus on communication and the expression of feelings. I therefore look at the role of counselling in schools, not from a specifically psychodynamic view but from a more eclectic one. This includes touching on specialist counselling, on the use of counselling-type skills in the teacher's day-to-day work and on peer counselling. The chapter then examines ways of encouraging communication and the expression of emotions and cathartic experiences through the curriculum.

Psychodynamic approaches

Psychodynamic approaches developed in many respects from Freudian psychoanalysis (see a brief summary of psychoanalysis in Freud, (2003 [1940]), and often still include features that are recognisably Freudian. The term 'psychodynamic' has been described as referring to 'emotional conflict or conflicts taking place within a person's internal, unconscious world or mind' (Ayers and Prytys, 2002, p. 168). Such approaches may include:

◆ the notion of unconscious drives of which the individual is unaware and the possible impact of these in personal adjustment;
◆ the cathartic release of emotions and emotional conflicts;
◆ the development of internal conflicts and their possible resolution;

♦ recognition of the importance of communication between and the relationship between the individual and the therapist.

Causal factors

Causal factors of BESD from the psychodynamic view may relate to unconscious drives and emotional conflict. Early childhood experiences are considered to exert a powerful influence on later emotional development.

Identification and assessment

The identification of pupils with BESD within a psychodynamic approach involves the recognition of behaviour and feelings that are incompatible with stable and fulfilling personal development. A specialist would consider that these manifestations are explainable in terms of psychodynamic theory. Interpretations of unconscious processes indicated by resistances, dreams, defence mechanisms and other factors may contribute to the assessment. An important method of assessment is the clinical interview.

Interventions

Therapies

Interventions drawing on a psychodynamic perspective include play therapy, music therapy, art therapy, drama therapy and movement therapy. Each in different degrees and in different ways may draw on psychodynamic approaches. Addresses and details can be found at the end of the book for:

♦ The Association of Play Therapists;
♦ The Association of Professional Music Therapists;
♦ The British Association of Art Therapists;
♦ The British Association of Drama Therapists;
♦ The Association for Dance Movement Therapy UK.

Play therapy

The Association of Play Therapists provides a summary of play therapy:

> Play therapy is the dynamic process between child and play therapist, in which the child explores, at his or her own pace and with his or her agenda, those issues past and current, conscious and unconscious, that are affecting the child's life in the present. The child's inner resources are enabled by the therapeutic alliance to bring about growth and change. Play therapy is child centred, in which play is the primary medium and speech is the secondary medium. Play therapy encompasses many approaches but the foundation of all approaches is child centred.
> (Association of Play Therapists, Code of Ethics, January 1996)

Play therapy may take place in the child's home, in school or in a clinic and the therapist encourages the child to play freely with materials that facilitate expression and aid the imagination. Materials might include puppets, miniature objects and paints. The child expresses feelings and fantasies through play and the therapist may see the child's concerns in certain themes that may occur.

Approaches may be directive or non-directive. In directive approaches, the therapist structures the play situation and impinges upon the child's unconscious in a purposeful way. This aims to help the child cope better with present feelings rather than explore early difficult experiences. Non-directive approaches have an underlying assumption that at some level the child is able to resolve her own problems. Reflective listening is used, in which the therapist reflects back to the child the feelings that are being expressed in the play. A range of approaches to play therapy is described in the book, *Counselling Children* (Geldard and Geldard, 1997).

Music therapy

Music therapy involves a therapist enabling a client to interact and to develop insight into behaviour and emotional difficulties via music. Sessions may take place in a day or private centre, a special school or a hospital and may be provided by a music therapist employed by the health, social or education services. The development of the relationship between the client and the music therapist is a vital aspect of music therapy and the making of music is the basis of the communication within this relationship. Sessions may be for an individual child or for a group and typically the therapist and the client(s) are involved in playing music, singing and listening.

The aim is to help the client make positive changes in behaviour and emotional well-being, to increase self-awareness and self-esteem and to improve the quality of the client's life. Feelings can be expressed and released non-verbally and this is perhaps particularly important for children who find verbal communication difficult. Most music therapy students are accepted on to postgraduate training courses after having achieved a diploma or graduation from a college of music or a university degree. (See also Bunt and Hoskyns, 2002.)

Art therapy

Art therapy involves the use of art materials to enable a client to express him- or herself and reflect on what is produced in the presence of an art therapist, the aim being to enable personal growth.

Because part of the communication between the therapist and the client involves the artefact, art therapy can be especially useful for children and young people who find it difficult to express their feelings and thoughts verbally.

Many art therapists have knowledge of psychodynamic theory, enabling them to work with conscious and unconscious material arising in the therapeutic sessions. Art therapy is provided in a safe environment such as a centre, a school or a hospital and may employ a variety of materials such as paint or clay. The therapy involves the therapist encouraging the client(s) to respond to what is being created. Suppressed feelings may be brought out and acknowledged.

Art therapists usually have a first degree in art and design (but occasionally may have another degree) and then follow a course leading to a postgraduate diploma over two years (full-time) or three years (part-time). Among employers of art therapists are the National Health Service, education services, social services and charities, or the therapist may be self-employed. For further information see Case and Daley (1992) and Edwards (2004).

Drama therapy

Drama therapy encourages clients to experience their physical nature, and to look again at their attitudes, values and feelings and to try out different ways of acting and behaving. Drama is used as a therapeutic process to encourage and develop creativity, insight and personal growth.

Among the settings in which a drama therapist works are schools, services for people with learning difficulties and private practice. To qualify as a drama therapist, after a degree or other relevant professional qualification, the student follows a postgraduate training course. Drama therapy is considered to be able to make a powerful contribution to raising a child's self-esteem and helping him understand and deal with emotions (e.g. McFarlane, 2005).

Drama therapy may work with an individual or with groups. Teachers and counsellors in the context of therapeutic work overseen by a therapist may use some of the techniques of drama therapy. Where role-play is used children are enabled to express powerful feelings and learn from externalising the experience. The roles may be the children being themselves, taking the part of other people in their lives or playing the part of symbolic characters.

Movement therapy

Among the benefits of movement therapy is that it offers the opportunity to express feelings and to experience a cathartic release of emotions. Confidence and self-esteem may be enhanced as the child's physical skills improve. Creative dance is a form of movement therapy. (See also Jones, 2004.)

Nurture groups

Psychoanalyst John Bowlby developed a theory of attachment, relating it to the biological survival of the species, that secures the infant's safety in a loving environment (Bowlby, 1965, 1969, 1973, 1980). Signals from the infant such as smiling are considered to be innate and help ensure that others respond to the infant's needs. In the so-called 'pre-attachment' phase, from birth to about six weeks, the infant does not appear to mind the presence of an unfamiliar adult as long as the infant's needs are met. But from six weeks to six months, in the 'attachment in the making' phase, the infant displays different behaviour to unknown adults and shows pleasure in the company of the main caregiver, usually the mother.

From six months to about two years is an 'attachment phase' in which the child shows separation anxiety if the familiar adult leaves. It seems that the child can grasp that the adult continues to exist even though he or she may be out of sight. The child actively seeks the company of the main caregiver. This leads to the phase of forming a reciprocal relationship from about the age of 18 months onwards. The formation of this reciprocal relationship is thought to be important for both interpersonal communication and stable emotional development.

Different forms of attachment are identified. Insecure attachment can be in two forms: anxious-avoidance and anxious-ambivalent. In anxious-avoidance, carers avoid comforting the child, leading to the child avoiding others. Anxious-ambivalent relationships are associated with carers being inconsistent in providing comfort for the child, leading to children clinging to others but being susceptible to anger. In dependent attachment, the child shows dependency and a lack of sense of personal identity. With disorganised attachment, resistance and avoidance behaviours are evident and shown by the child being unsure whether to approach or avoid the carer. The nature of the attachment is thought to influence the development of adult relationships with others. Children having experienced insecure attachments are more likely to experience emotional difficulties (Holmes, 1993).

Nurture groups have their foundations in the attachment theory of John Bowlby. The relationship between the child and the adult is important to the child developing a sense of self. Social development is encouraged focusing on the emotional aspects of the interactions between the child and the caregiver. A nurture group is a form of early intervention for children whose emotional, social and behavioural needs are unable to be met in the mainstream classroom, the intention being to return the children to the mainstream classroom as soon as appropriate. It is thought that these children have not had the early learning experiences that would enable them to function appropriately, both socially and emotionally, for their age. A nurture group therefore emphasises emotional growth and offers a range of experiences in an environment that provides security, clear boundaries, predictable routines and planned repetitive opportunities for learning (Boxall, 2002). The nurture group might consist of a teacher and a learning support assistant who 'model' positive behaviour and social skills in a structure that is commensurate with the developmental level of the child. There may be ten to twelve children in the group. Through this process, the child is considered to be able to develop an attachment to the adult, receive approval and experience positive outcomes.

Counselling

General framework

It will be remembered that psychodynamic approaches concern 'emotional conflict or conflicts taking place within a person's internal, unconscious world or mind' (Ayers and Prytys, 2002, p. 168). Such approaches may include recognition of the importance of communication and the relationship between the individual and the therapist. In many approaches to counselling there is a similar emphasis.

Counselling has been defined as:

> A relationship in which counsellors or helpers assist clients to understand themselves and their problems better. Where appropriate, they then use various interventions to enable clients to feel, think, communicate and act more

effectively. Approaches to counselling practice differ according to theoretical orientation.

(Nelson-Jones, 2005, p. 330, glossary)

In a school context, it has been said that counselling, '. . . involves helping students individually or in small groups to deal with the concerns or difficulties they are experiencing' (Hornby *et al.*, 2003, p. 4). Also, Hornby and colleagues suggest, drawing on other authors, different levels of counselling in schools. Level 1 involves using counselling skills in the classroom to provide 'a positive learning environment' and raise pupils' self-esteem. Level 2 refers to the use of counselling skills by the form tutor to help pupils 'solve day-to-day problems' and to facilitate group activities within a personal, social, health and citizenship education (PSHCE) programme. At level 3, individual or small-group counselling is available from a 'trained specialist within the school' who might be a school counsellor, a guidance counsellor, or a member of staff with a pastoral leadership role. Level 4 involves using referral procedures to 'help pupils access professionals outside the school', such as a psychologist or psychiatrist who would provide specialist counselling help (p. 4).

Specialist counselling

This section is concerned particularly with what would be described as levels 3 and 4 of the above framework, that is, counselling from a trained specialist within the school or a counselling professional outside the school. In terms of provision for SEN this would often relate to School Action and School Action Plus interventions or interventions considered suitable for a pupil with a statement of SEN.

A possible model for counselling in school, which can include specialist interventions, is suggested by Hornby and colleagues (Hornby *et al.*, 2003, e.g. pp. 17–21) and involves three stages. It is not an exclusively psychodynamic model but is described as, 'a developmental counselling model, based on humanistic principles, set within a psychosocial framework' (p. 17). The three stages concern: exploration, intervention and empowering.

Exploration entails establishing a therapeutic relationship (communicating to the pupil empathy, genuineness and respect), exploring concerns and assessing the situation. Intervention may involve approaches such as play therapy, problem-solving and other techniques. Empowering concerns supporting action programmes that have been devised, perhaps using praise or teaching the pupil to be more assertive; consolidating changes for example by reminding the pupil of the progress he has made; and enabling self-actualisation, perhaps by teaching life skills (p. 19).

Counselling-type skills in everyday communication

The previous section mentioned different levels of counselling in schools and concentrated on levels 3 and 4 (Hornby *et al.*, 2003, p. 4). This present section is concerned particularly with what would be described as levels 1 and 2 of the above framework. It will be remembered that level 1 concerned using counselling skills in the classroom to provide 'a positive learning environment' and raise pupils' self-esteem. Level 2 referred to the use of counselling skills by the form tutor to help pupils 'solve day-to-day problems' and to facilitate group activities within a PSHCE programme.

Listening skills are essential and include the appropriate use of eye contact, adopting an 'open' bodily posture and remaining relaxed (e.g. Hornby *et al.*, pp. 25–6). Sometimes counselling-related skills can be used effectively by the teacher or learning support assistant in day-to-day contacts with pupils with BESD (e.g. McNamara and Moreton, 2001, pp. 32–4). Paraphrasing and reflective listening involve reflecting back what the child or young person has said and often lead to the child elaborating and giving more information about his concerns or about how he perceives a situation. The following exchange might take place in an agreed counselling session or more informally at the pupil's desk:

Pupil: 'Maths is rubbish!'
Teacher: 'So you don't like maths any more?'
Pupil: 'It's rubbish. I can't even do sums that I used to do a year ago.'
Teacher: 'You are finding the work difficult at the moment then?'

Although such an approach has been parodied ('Good morning', 'So you think it's a good morning do you?'), used skilfully it can be a powerful way of encouraging communication and getting into the detail of a problem. A related technique that may be used in a counselling session and in day-to-day communication is seeking to confirm an unspoken feeling ('Is what you are saying that you are finding being outside in the playground difficult it's making you feel scared?').

Stating one's own feelings can be used when an alternative might involve criticising the pupil's behaviour, as well as in other situations. To a pupil used to constantly hearing streams of criticism, it can be a powerful message. Stating one's feelings of course must be genuine. ('I feel sad when I hear you say that you don't care that you have hurt Jennie. I know that you like her and I am wondering if something has happened that you might want to talk about.')

Using new patterns of language (sometimes referred to as 'scripts') such as blame-free statements is helpful to aid communication. Related to this is a three-part script (from the work of Gordan, 1974). It involves:

♦ a description of the pupil's behaviour;
♦ a statement about the teacher's behaviour;
♦ a statement about the consequences for the teacher of the pupil's behaviour.

Peer counselling

In peer counselling, trained and supervised students carry out 'interpersonal helping tasks' (Hornby *et al.*, 2003, p. 71) with clients of a similar age who may have referred themselves or who may have been referred by others. These helping tasks include 'listening, offering support, suggesting alternatives' (p. 71).

An example of a whole school anti-bullying policy involving peer helpers was devised by a secondary school in Stafford, England (Cartright, 1996, pp. 97–105). Student peer counsellors are selected for such qualities as personal and social maturity and their commitment to the programme. Members of staff experienced in counselling train them and this involves developing listening skills, identifying problems, problem-solving and referral.

Encouraging communication and the expression of emotions through the curriculum

Communication and the curriculum

Some subjects of the curriculum encourage personal expression and communication. While the opportunity to communicate concerns or to express feelings is clearly important to all pupils, it may particularly benefit pupils with BESD. Subjects encouraging the expression of feelings and communication generally are aspects of English such as discussions and debates, drama, play, physical education, art and music. Where schools are educating children with BESD, they may review the curriculum to ensure that the potential benefits of such subjects are being realised through having sufficient curriculum time and through ensuring the content is likely to encourage communication and the expression of feelings.

The example of art therapy may be taken to draw a distinction between communication and therapeutic intervention. The differences between art therapy and arts education are many, although there are areas of overlap where there are considered to be 'client-centred' art therapies and arts education. However, art therapies have personal aims, a therapeutic agenda, do not entail instruction, and involve the monitoring of artistic/aesthetic changes. Arts education has artistic and aesthetic aims, an artistic agenda, involves instruction, and seeks the improvement of artistic quality. Art therapists and art teachers are differently trained, qualified and professionally registered. While art therapists can work in collaboration with teachers, it is important that art teachers do not seek to become substitute art therapists. It is advised that teacher-led programmes anticipate and prepare for 'unexpected disclosures' through having specialist advice available and knowing appropriate referral procedures.

Cathartic experiences and the curriculum

In his early theorising, Sigmund Freud used the adjective 'cathartic' to apply to the therapeutic methods he developed between 1880 and 1895 when he was using techniques related to mesmerism, a precursor of hypnotism (Freud and Breuer, 1987 [1893–5]). The recovery of a repressed traumatic memory allowed the patient to 'abreact' the 'affects' associated with the memory in a powerful cathartic discharge of emotion. Freud's colleague Joseph Breuer, treating 'Anna O.' using hypnosis, discovered that, if his patient could recall the first moment when a particular hysterical symptom appeared, and experienced again the accompanying emotion, the symptom disappeared. Breuer called this form of treatment 'catharsis'. Hypnosis enabled the patient to recall the forgotten origins of the particular symptoms. The reminiscences were not easy to access by conscious recall and they were painful or shameful. This suggested a mental mechanism that pushed back unpleasant memories from consciousness (repression). Freud suggested that the rejected emotion, which had been repressed because it was unable to become conscious and to be discharged, gave rise to neurotic symptoms.

While Freud ceased to employ such devices, cathartic methods are still used in some psychotherapeutic approaches, including psychodrama where role-play may be used to seek to create a release from internal emotional conflicts.

Certain curriculum subjects and areas are cathartic in a less technical sense in that they are thought to encourage a release of emotions that is considered broadly beneficial. These subjects include drama, play, physical education, art and music. Typical of the positive effects of aspects of these subjects is the feeling of having released pent-up energy. Where schools are educating children with BESD, they may review the curriculum to ensure that the potential benefits of such subjects are being realised through having sufficient curriculum time and in terms of having subject content likely to encourage emotional release. Particular care will need to be taken with sports because there are differences of opinion about whether participating in such activities leads to a cathartic release of emotion that is likely to reduce aggression or whether such activities might in fact increase violent tendencies.

THINKING POINTS

Readers may wish to consider, with reference to a particular school:

◆ the potential for the use (or better use) of specialist therapists for pupils with BESD;
◆ for primary schools, the potential of nurture groups as an early intervention strategy;
◆ the extent to which school provision can contribute to communicative and cathartic experiences that may have a positive effect on the behaviour and well-being of pupils with BESD;
◆ the degree to which counselling-type skills can be further developed as part of the teachers' day-to-day work and how the effect of this might be monitored.

KEY TEXTS

Hornby, G., Hall, C. and Hall, E. (2003) *Counselling Pupils in Schools: Skills and Strategies for Teachers*, London, RoutledgeFalmer.

This book covers a wide range of skills and strategies relating to counselling and guidance within the school context. The term counselling is used broadly (as indicated in the suggested four levels discussed in the present chapter) to range from using counselling skills in day-to-day situations to referring a pupil for specialist counselling.

Jones, P. (2004) *The Arts Therapies: A Revolution in Healthcare*, London, Routledge.

This includes sections on art therapy, music therapy, drama therapy and dance therapy. Part five focuses on the client–therapist relationship.

Chapter 6

Attention deficit hyperactivity disorder (ADHD)

INTRODUCTION

This chapter defines and describes ADHD and outlines approaches to its identification and assessment. The prevalence of ADHD is considered and factors associated with ADHD are examined in terms of genetic, physiological, psychological and environmental influences and their possible interaction. Interventions with pupils with ADHD are discussed beginning with general approaches that are also used with pupils having BESD. Next, approaches that are more specific to pupils with ADHD are examined under the related headings of: the classroom environment and classroom management; behaviour and communication; teaching and learning approaches; and skills teaching. Medication and diet are also considered. Finally, by way of summary, the chapter outlines strategies used in a particular LEA.

Defining and describing ADHD

The term ADHD emerged from earlier attempts to describe inattentive and overactive behaviour and is defined in the *Diagnostic and Statistical Manual of the American Psychiatric Association (DSM-IV-TR)* (APA, 2000, pp. 85–93). Similar criteria published by the World Health Organization (1990) define 'Hyperkinetic Disorder'. ADHD is understood in relation to inattention, hyperactivity and impulsivity.

In the *Diagnostic and Statistical Manual of Mental Disorders (DSM-IV-TR)* (APA, 2000, pp. 85–93) there are nine criteria relating to *inattention* including, 'often fails to give close attention to details or makes careless mistakes in schoolwork, work or other activities' and 'often has difficulty sustaining attention in tasks or play activities'. There are six criteria concerning *hyperactivity,* such as 'is often on the go' or often acts as if 'driven by a motor'. The three criteria concerning *impulsivity* include 'often has difficulty awaiting turn' (p. 92).

The diagnostic criteria state that six or more of the nine criteria for inattention *or* six or more of the nine criteria for hyperactivity-impulsivity should have persisted for at least six months to an extent that is 'maladaptive and inconsistent with developmental level'. Four further criteria must be met including that 'some impairment from the symptoms is present in two or more settings . . .' (such as at school and at home) and that 'Some hyperactive-impulsive or inattentive symptoms that caused impairment were present before age 7 years' (p. 92).

It will be seen that it is possible for a child to meet the diagnostic criteria if he manifests the indications in different combinations. For example, he may show: six or more of the nine criteria for inattention or all six criteria for hyperactivity or all three criteria for impulsivity and three or more criteria for hyperactivity. These will influence whether the difficulty is seen as predominantly inattention, or hyperactivity or impulsivity with hyperactivity.

If behaviour that appears to be ADHD is evidently related to external problems, it is unlikely that it is ADHD. The teacher or other concerned adult should seek to help the child remove or deal with the factors that appear to be precipitating the behaviour, then reconsider the assessment.

Identification and assessment

Criteria such as those referred to in the previous section are used in identifying and assessing ADHD as part of assessment procedures that ideally involve bringing together information from different sources (the child, the parent, the teacher and others) on how the child functions in different circumstances and settings.

Qualitative assessments can include interviewing, or using questionnaires for the child, members of the family, peers and teachers. Quantitative assessments may involve psychological, medical and educational information. This may involve using standardised tests of cognitive performance; computerised tests of attention and vigilance; and a medical examination including tests of hearing and vision (Cooper and O'Regan, 2001, p. 19).

There are overlaps with other aspects of BESD and ADHD. Below is a list of difficulties followed by an estimate in brackets of the percentage of children within that group that have ADHD:

- ◆ Antisocial or delinquent behaviour (25 per cent)
- ◆ Oppositional and defiant behaviour (50–60 per cent)
- ◆ Conduct disorder (45 per cent)
- ◆ Emotional problems (50+ per cent)
- ◆ Severe social skills problems (50+ per cent)

(p. 20, adapted)

The *Goodman Strengths and Difficulties Questionnaire* (Goodman, 1997, 1999) is a norm-referenced behaviour rating scale having sub-scales for: emotional problems; peer difficulties; hyperactivity; conduct problems; and pro-social behaviour. Intended to apply to children aged 4 to 16 years, the questionnaire has a version for parents, teachers and pupils aged 11 to 16 years. It is used as a screening device for groups of children but also as a diagnostic/assessment tool for individual pupils with ADHD (Hill and Cameron, 1999). The *Goodman SDQ* can be used to evaluate a pupil's progress or regress over time, and it can be used to help assess the effectiveness of interventions. Also, when comparisons are made between the perceptions of teachers, pupils and parents, this can encourage insights into the behaviour of the pupil at school and at home.

Another example of a scale relating to ADHD and aiming to assess a broad range of behaviour difficulties is the *Connors' Rating Scales (Revised)* (Connors, 1996). The age range covered is 3 to 17 years and there are versions for parents, the teacher and the pupil (an adolescent self-report form). The scales are administered individually with the long version taking about 45 minutes to complete and the short version taking about 15 minutes.

Prevalence

Prevalence in relation to SEN refers to the number of children with a particular type of SEN in a certain population over a specified period. Incidences are usually expressed as the number of children per live births in a given year. Prevalence relates to incidence in the sense that prevalence is determined by the incidence of a condition and its duration (see also Farrell, 2003, pp. 129–30).

In the United States of America, it has been estimated that about 5 to 7 per cent of school children are affected with ADHD. In the United Kingdom the estimates range from 1 per cent to 20 per cent with the most usual estimate being between 1 per cent and 7 per cent. This may relate to the strictness of the diagnostic criteria, especially the location of cut-off points, although the very wide range cannot inspire either parents or professionals with confidence that there is clear consensus as to what constitutes ADHD. The proportion of children considered to have ADHD among those identified as having BESD is much higher than in the population of children in general. For example, in a school for pupils with 'emotional and behavioural difficulties' there were judged to be 70 per cent with ADHD (Place *et al.*, 2000). The ratio of boys to girls is thought to be 8:1 or 10:1 (e.g. Ayers and Prytys, 2002, p. 28). The higher ratio of boys to girls applies to children considered to have predominantly hyperactive behaviour, predominantly impulsive behaviours and those with both.

Possible causal factors

Possible causal factors include genetic, physiological, psychological and environmental influences.

ADHD is more common in the biological relatives of children having ADHD than it is in the biological relatives of children who do not. Twin studies show a greater incidence of ADHD among identical twins than non-identical twins. Studies have compared the incidence of ADHD among children and parents who are biologically related with that of children of parents where the child is adopted. These indicate a greater probability of ADHD appearing in parents and children when they are biologically related (Tannock, 1998). This suggests that biological factors may predispose children to ADHD.

It has been suggested that ADHD may be related to dysfunction in the brain's neurotransmission system, which is responsible for making connections between different parts of the brain. Brain imaging research has shown for individuals with ADHD abnormalities in the frontal lobes of the brain where systems responsible for regulating attention are centred. In 20 to 30 per cent of instances, particularly in severe cases, of ADHD, such physiological factors are caused by brain disease, brain injury or exposure to toxins such as alcohol or drugs. To the extent that stimulant drugs such as methylphenidate (Ritalin) are effective in reducing hyper-activity, this may indicate that hyperactivity results from an under-arousal of the mid-brain, which leads to insufficient inhibition of movements and sensations. It is thought that stimulant drugs stimulate the mid-brain sufficiently to suppress the overactivity.

A psychological theory of ADHD is that there is a dysfunction of the psycho-logical mechanism for self-regulation so that a child with ADHD has more difficulty than is typical in delaying a behavioural response. Another view is that characteristics of individuals having ADHD lead to difficulties with 'executive functions'. These executive functions involve the mental filtering and checking processes that an individual uses to make decisions about how to behave. They involve using inner speech, which may, for example, evaluate information held in the working memory; taking one's emotional state into account; and recalling knowledge from situations similar to the one in which one finds oneself (Barkley, 1997).

Environmental factors, including family influences, may mediate other factors in influencing the probability of ADHD. For example, in one study, a child with ADHD was more likely to have a mother with symptoms of anxiety or who had been recently seriously depressed than were other children. Where a child had ADHD and was also considered to have conduct disorder and oppositional defiant disorder, the father tended to score higher on measures of 'neuroticism' and lower on measures of 'agreeableness' than fathers in a comparison group (Nigg and Hinshaw, 1998).

In a bio-psycho-social model, a tentative picture of ADHD may be formed from considering the factors that may be implicated. There may be differences in the brain morphology of individuals with ADHD and those who do not have the condition. These brain differences may lead to cognitive differences in terms of how easily an individual can inhibit responses to stimuli. A particular child's circumstances, and the other skills and capacities that she has, are likely to have an influence on whether these cognitive factors lead to difficulties that might be considered as ADHD.

Interventions

Reviewing approaches that work for pupils with BESD in general

Approaches that tend to work for pupils with BESD may be applicable to pupils identified as having ADHD. Among interventions that can contribute are those associated with systems approaches, especially aspects encouraging close home–school working. Psychotherapeutic interventions are not considered within present understandings of ADHD but distantly related approaches such as using an advocate or mentor are useful. Among cognitive interventions that can be helpful is self-talk.

Behavioural approaches can be effective, for example in reinforcing social skills, as indicated later. Behavioural programmes are most effective when used as a supplement to suitable educational provision rather than being seen as the main focus for intervention with pupils with ADHD. Where possible, behavioural programmes should emphasise the positive behaviours required rather than the negative ones to be discouraged. Among interventions that can be effective are: time out, token economies, contracts and punishment (Cooper and O'Regan, 2001, p. 53). Also, to the extent that aspects of BESD such as 'conduct disorder' accompany ADHD, approaches that work with BESD more generally can be adapted as necessary.

The classroom environment and classroom management

Allowing optimum breaks from class work appears to help reduce inattention and allow for the need for activity associated with impulsiveness. There is evidence of a relationship between having what appears to be insufficient time for breaks from class work and increases in pupils' disruption and inattention (Pellegrini and Horvat, 1995; Pellegrini *et al.*, 1996). This has been interpreted as suggesting 'frequent short periods of physical activity', for example perhaps 10 minutes every 40 minutes for primary school children (Cooper and O'Regan, 2001, p. 39).

Some research has indicated that pupils with ADHD can sustain effort and concentration in structured and controlled situations where the activity is stimulating but find it particularly difficult to return to an activity once distracted (e.g. Borger and Van der Meer, 2000). To the extent that this can be generalised, it follows that a learning environment that is likely to benefit pupils with ADHD is one that is structured and controlled; where the learning task is stimulating; and where distractions are minimised. It can help the pupil with ADHD if the teacher can sometimes respond to pupil comments that may be impulsive and unconnected with the teacher's chosen theme and direction of the lesson. If the teacher can use such a response to engage the pupil further yet still carry the lesson in the desired direction, the pupil is more likely to be motivated and interested. This of course is one of the skills of effective teaching for all pupils.

Given that pupils with ADHD tend to be easily distracted, the teachers should consider carefully the layout of the classroom and the general nature of the classroom environment. A pupil with ADHD is likely to be able to concentrate better if seated away from windows, displays and other potential distractions. At times, the pupil with ADHD (and others) may benefit from working in an area facing a wall with portable partitions on either side. These would be in a position where the teacher can see the pupil (from the back) and monitor whether the pupil is carrying out the required activity (e.g. Cooper and O'Regan, 2001, p. 47). Where discussion is part of a lesson, the pupil with ADHD may be less distracted working in a pair rather than in a larger group, although this is not to say that opportunities to develop the skills of participating in larger groups should be denied.

Providing clear routines that help him deal in a step-by-step way with the requirements of the school day and sessions within the day can reduce a pupil's difficulty with attention and organising information. Routine aids that are used for all pupils are likely to help, such as weekly and daily timetables and previews of what is planned for a lesson and reviews of what has been achieved. For a pupil with ADHD, complicated timetabling arrangements are likely to require particular support. Among particularly confusing features might be: 'rotating' termly sessions, for example of different strands of design and technology (resistant materials, food technology, textiles); or blocked subjects such as a 'French week'. Secure routines are intended to help support a child with impulsive worries and thoughts and feelings of insecurity so that the pupil knows what to expect. But the secure predictability of routine should not become over-rigid. The intention is that the routines in time help the pupil to internalise controls. Visual reminders of a task may be posted on the pupil's desk or on a wall in a partitioned area. These reminders may be in the form of a picture or a series of pictures to help the pupil remember the sequencing of the task.

Encouraging the pupil to develop a positive understanding and use of duration tends to help reduce inattention and perhaps impulsivity. The teacher can set tasks with clear time limits that are conveyed to the pupil rather than having open-ended tasks. This can help the pupil structure time better in aiming to complete the task. A clock or sand timer can assist some pupils to recognise the passage of time involved in an activity providing the time allocated for the task realistically matches the requirements of the task and the pupil's capacity to concentrate adequately for the specified duration.

Behaviour and communication

Biofeedback involves the pupil monitoring the physiological manifestations of his own psychological process. An instrument is used that responds to physiological changes and emits a signal such as a sound tone. This in turn enables the person to respond to the physiological changes and to try and control them. For example, in the case of hyperactivity, muscle tone is monitored. The biofeedback signal is activated when muscle tension is high and this enables the child to become aware of this and to use relaxation exercises to reduce the tension and relax. More generally, pupils may be taught to monitor their own behaviour and prompt themselves to keep track of how they are responding.

In helping the pupil to manage his behaviour, the teacher may use unobtrusive methods. These aim to encourage attention and concentration and to discourage impulsivity and overactivity. For example, the pupil may be seated in a position so that the teacher can see whether or not the pupil is giving attention. Attention can then be encouraged as necessary, for example through the use of previously agreed unobtrusive signs such as displaying a coloured card or the administration of rewards.

Through discussion and sensitive 'feedback' on behaviour, a pupil can be helped to recognise various feelings such as frustration, anger or disappointment and develop a vocabulary to describe them. The pupil can be taught ways of communicating these feelings. For example, previously agreed signals might be used such as cards of specified colours to signal to the teacher that the pupil is finding a situation or a task too difficult to deal with.

Teaching and learning approaches

To the extent that a pupil with ADHD favours concrete experience (over more abstract conceptualisation) and active, experiential, experimental learning (over reflective observation) (Wallace and Crawford, 1994), such experiences and approaches to learning can be optimised. This indicates that a pupil with ADHD is likely to learn best in activities like drama, role-play and practical activities such as those in science and design and technology. Also, subjects that normally involve abstract conceptualisation and reflective observation can be approached initially through concrete experience and active learning and can be supported by the continuation of elements of the concrete and experiential. This recognises the requirement for activity in pupils with ADHD and helps attention and concentration because the physical and the concrete form the medium of learning and at the same time act as visual, auditory and kinaesthetic prompts and aids.

For all pupils, and perhaps particularly where pupils find attention and involvement difficult, learning activities should: be interesting and stimulating; be clearly defined with explicit learning objectives; and give early experience of success, later leading on to more complex and demanding tasks.

The teacher should give clear guidance and instructions in manageable chunks that are reinforced as necessary by written and pictorial aids. She should ensure that the pupil understands, for example by questioning him or by asking him to put into his own words what is required. Such aids and checking of comprehension help the pupil understand and follow sequences of activities, which is important because pupils with ADHD tend to find sequences and sequencing difficult. This all helps the pupil improve his organisation.

Social skills teaching and developing compensatory skills

Teaching and reinforcing, through praise and other means, social skills, which may be lacking or underdeveloped in a child with ADHD, can be helpful. Some approaches in connection with this were mentioned in the chapter on behavioural approaches to BESD in general. The skills taught include conversational skills such as timing and showing interest in what others say. Methods used to develop these skills include discussion, role-play, and staff or capable pupils modelling desired behaviours both in day-to-day contact and in structured sessions (Hargie *et al.*, 1994). Modelling of suitable behaviour by capable peers can be a powerful aid to social skills learning.

The teacher can assist the pupil in developing skills that may help compensate for difficulties associated with impulsiveness and overactivity by playing to the pupil's strengths. For example, the pupil may be given opportunities to perform well in energetic sports or in drama activities requiring improvisation or more generally in activity-based learning.

Medication and diet

In the United States of America, around 90 per cent of pupils with ADHD receive medication of some kind (Greenhill, 1998). In the United Kingdom, about 10 per cent of children with ADHD are estimated to receive medication (Munder and Arcelus, 1999) with less than 6 per cent being administered methylphenidate (Ritalin) (National Institute of Clinical Excellence, 2000).

Stimulant drugs such as Ritalin can be effective. This suggests that the hyperactivity results from an under-arousal of the mid-brain, which causes insufficient inhibition of movements and sensations. Stimulant drugs appear to stimulate the mid-brain sufficiently to suppress the overactivity. Stimulants can therefore act by improving the child's ability to concentrate when hyperactive behaviours are inhibited. Electrophysiological investigations (using neuroimaging) have indicated that, for children taking Ritalin, stimulus recognition is improved in terms of improved attention to auditory and visual stimuli (Seifert *et al*, 2003).

Medication is used to try to improve the child's receptiveness and so enable him to learn more appropriate behaviours and skills such as better self-regulation. Medication is used in combination with other approaches such as behavioural interventions (British Psychological Society, 2000). The school and the home monitor the effects of any medication and it is widely accepted that a thorough assessment is necessary before medication is used. Also, when drugs are used, their effects should be carefully and continuously monitored. For parents, decisions about whether medication may be used may be informed by consideration of possible side effects and whether they are convinced that the medication is likely to make the child more available for learning (e.g. Farrell, 2004, p. 52). Ritalin is administered orally in tablet form, usually in the mornings and afternoons, and it is not used with children under 4 years old. It is contraindicated where there is a highrisk of cardiovascular disease, or tic disorders such as Tourette's syndrome. Possible side effects that have been reported are insomnia and a temporary loss of appetite.

Turning to the question of diet, while food allergy is popularly believed to be a common cause of hyperactivity, research studies indicate it is involved only rarely. Among dietary interventions is the Feingold diet. Its rationale is that some research has linked food additives to allergies and that hyperactivity may be a symptom of an allergic reaction. The diet seeks to eliminate the intake of salicylates found in certain fresh fruits and vegetables, food flavourings, food colourings and in some preservatives. It appears to benefit a small proportion of children who are considered 'hyperactive'.

Hampshire LEA guidance strategies

A list of strategies developed by Hampshire County Council (1996) intended for pupils with ADHD covers some of the points already raised in this chapter and echoed in previous chapters and may act as a helpful overview. The strategies concern inattention, excessive motor activity, poor organisation and planning, impulsiveness, non-compliance, difficulties with peers and poor self-esteem.

For example, 'inattention' strategies include providing feedback on behaviour that is consistent with established behaviour modification principles (frequent, immediate and consistent) and redirecting the pupil back to the task. Other tactics are to sit the pupil away from distractions, to provide cues to keep the pupil on task, for example by using a private signal, and, for taking tests, to provide an environment with fewer distractions than the usual classroom. In presenting tasks, the teacher should keep the format of worksheet and similar resources simple and avoid supplying extraneous pictures or other visual distractions that are unrelated to the task. (The point about visual distractions should not be taken to suggest condoning an impoverished environment but to ensure that visual aids are clearly relevant to the work in hand.)

Concerning 'excessive motor activity', strategies include allowing opportunities for the pupil to move around the room, planning in advance for transitions (changes of lesson or activity), establishing rules and supervising closely. Regarding 'poor organisation and planning', the teacher can provide a checklist (that is kept easily accessible and visible) of steps to be taken in following directions or checking that a task is correctly completed. Also, the teacher can try to ensure that assignments are given one at a time. Turning to 'impulsiveness', strategies include teaching verbal mediation skills to reduce impulsive behaviour by modelling, including practising 'stop/listen/look/think/answer/do'. Also, the teacher can increase immediate rewards and consequences.

For 'non-compliance', the teacher can give immediate feedback about acceptable and unacceptable behaviour. With regard to 'difficulties with peers', the teacher can ensure that suitable social behaviour is praised. Finally, in relation to 'poor self-esteem', the teacher and others can focus on the pupil's talents and achievements.

It will be seen that these strategies are practical, relate to what ADHD is taken to mean and are conversant with broader approaches covered in earlier chapters of the present book, particularly in relation to behavioural, cognitive and systems perspectives.

THINKING POINTS

Readers may wish to consider:

◆ how valid and reliable are the arrangements in relation to their setting (LEA, school etc.) for identifying and assessing ADHD;

◆ the extent to which approaches related to BESD in general are used and could be further used for pupils with ADHD;

◆ the extent to which a range of well-thought-out approaches to pupils with ADHD are used and could be further developed.

KEY TEXTS

American Psychiatric Association (2000) *Diagnostic and Statistical Manual of Mental Disorders – Text Revision (DSM-IV-TR)* (4th edn), Washington DC, APA.

This manual sets out the criteria for a wide range of mental disorders including, as indicated in this chapter, those for ADHD. Another typology is the *International Classification of Functioning, Disability and Health*, published by the World Health Organization in Geneva in 2001.

Cooper, P. and O'Regan, F. J. (2001) *Educating Children with AD/HD*, London, RoutledgeFalmer.

> Part one of this book concerns 'understanding ADHD'. Part two covers principles and practices for intervention. Part three provides case studies of pupils with ADHD and other features that are presented as 'types' of ADHD, for example 'ADHD with detachment' and 'ADHD with obsessions'. Two appendices set out the 1994 'DSMIV Diagnostic Criteria for Attention-Deficit/ Hyperactivity Disorder' and 'ICD 10 F90 Hyperkinetic Disorder'.

Chapter 7

Conclusion

INTRODUCTION

This chapter first reiterates how different perspectives can illuminate provision for pupils with BESD by looking specifically at explanations of conduct disorder and anxiety. I then examine interventions in relation to the pupil's age and cognitive development; the different levels at which the interventions are supported (local authority, school, classroom); the compatibility of interventions; and approaches that bring together provision at LEA and school levels. Finally, I consider how interventions might be justified.

Different approaches focused on aspects of BESD

The importance of examining different perspectives in relation to BESD is emphasised by the fact that aspects of BESD can be understood and approached from these different viewpoints. For example, perspectives of and interventions related to conduct disorder draw on different standpoints.

A systems approach focusing on the family tends to see adolescent aggression as relating to family disorganisation with vague and ineffective boundaries and lax routines. The communications within the family may be confusing and lacking empathy and problems would tend to be 'solved' through coercion. Where both school and family systems are considered, conduct disorders would be additionally seen in a school context in which the pupil is likely not to be achieving well. Intervention might include family therapy. A cognitive-behavioural view would focus on cognitive deficits and distortions such as attributing hostile intent to people in neutral situations and poor problem-solving skills. Interventions would include training in problem-solving skills. From a behavioural point of view, contributing factors would be seen as antisocial behaviours being 'reinforced' through contact with delinquent peer groups and behaviour being modelled on poor exemplars, such as inconsistently harshly punitive parents and aggressive siblings or other peers. Retraining would be indicated as well as parent training in behaviour management. Psychodynamic explanations might look to poor super-ego functioning and insecure attachments in early childhood. It is likely that the appropriate intervention would be considered to be psychotherapy.

To take another example more briefly, anxiety might be regarded from a systems theory standpoint as relating to family factors such as anxious parents who elicit anxiety from other family members. Family crises and the way in which they are dealt with may activate anxiety in children. From the cognitive perspective, such factors as threat-oriented cognitive distortions would be seen as contributing to anxiety. Interventions could include challenging the irrational beliefs regarding danger and threats. Behavioural views would focus on conditioned fear and anxiety responses, which subsequent events had reinforced. Interventions might be phased exposure to the events and objects that provoked anxiety. Psychodynamic explanations might refer to the effects of the repression of unconscious morally abhorrent sexual or aggressive impulses.

Age and cognitive development

Some interventions are intended for pupils of a particular age, such as nurture groups, which are suitable for very young children as an early intervention, and play therapy, which also tends to be used with young children. On the other hand, monitoring one's behaviour as an intervention for pupils with ADHD is likely to be more effective for older pupils having some understanding of the purpose of self-monitoring. Some interventions assume a level of cognitive development that is age typical. Psychotherapeutic interventions that are predominantly verbal assume the child to be sufficiently articulate to communicate with the therapist and to respond to mainly verbally conveyed interventions. Other psychotherapeutic interventions do not depend so much on the child having an age-typical level of cognitive development. Play therapy and music therapy are examples, although, of course, they are also used with children whose cognitive development is typical of their chronological age.

'Levels' at which interventions apply

Interventions may have particular application or relevance at the level of the LEA, the school or the classroom. Interventions such as a systems approach across an LEA clearly depend on co-ordination and agreement at LEA level. The range of interventions available to a school is also often facilitated by LEA decisions, for example behaviour support staff or educational psychologists having experience and skills in behavioural techniques and offering support and training in these. The availability of specialist psychotherapeutic interventions will relate to the provision available through the local health service or sometimes trusts or charities. Schools sometimes employ such specialists directly.

While all approaches require the support of the school, some particularly depend on whole-school support. A token economy is more likely to work when embedded in a whole school, or a unit, than if it is attempted piecemeal in a single classroom.

Some interventions (given the support of the school) can be to a greater extent developed in individual classrooms. Aspects of behavioural approaches such as positive reinforcement of wanted behaviour work in primary classrooms where teachers spend most of the timetabled week with the same class. Circle time is sometimes used by one or two classes in a primary school and not in other classes.

Compatibility of interventions

Some interventions are compatible with others while some interventions are less so. A systems approach using a framework of intervention across an LEA would be compatible with most other approaches considered. This is because it is an example of a systems approach and valuable in its own right. But it can also help to ensure that systems/environmental explanations and aspects of what appear to be BESD are fully taken into account before other more 'within child' explanations and approaches are considered and developed.

If self-injurious behaviour or behaviour likely to harm others is a problem, it can be reduced by, for example, behavioural methods without necessarily closing the door to psychotherapeutic interventions to help ensure the expression and release of emotions and frustrations. Such combined approaches require careful planning and monitoring and the aims of the approaches will need to be clear, explicit and agreed by all concerned.

Towards an LEA, school and classroom topography for pupils with BESD

This book has considered various perspectives on BESD and the range of interventions that can be used at LEA, whole-school and classroom level, some drawing on outside support such as that from an educational psychologist. Given this, it may be helpful to look at an overview of how various elements of provision can link together.

One such overview (Ali *et al.*, 1997; Daniels and Williams, 2000) was indicated in Chapter 2: 'Systems approach'. It will be remembered that this involved a referral system linking such elements as classroom practice, the role of the behaviour co-ordinator, a BEP, IBPs and outside support.

McSherry (2001) describes a rather more structural approach. She presents a framework for intervention with pupils having 'challenging behaviour' and their integration. This framework, the Coping in Schools programme, focuses on various aspects:

1   *Previous experiences and their effects*
    Using a transactional model that emphasises previous experiences affecting present interactions.

2   *Teacher–pupil interactions*
    Involving cognitive-behavioural change to improve interventions and to change the way in which behaviour and its consequences are regarded.

3   *Involving parents and working closely with them*

4   *A whole school approach*
    Involving a range of support strategies such as learning mentors; referral to a within school learning support unit; PSPs; dual registration of pupils with a mainstream school; a pupil referral unit and so on.

5   *A whole LEA approach*
    For example using common forms of assessment.

(pp. 9–17 paraphrased)

The framework involves an approach to enabling the reintegration of pupils from a special school for children with BESD to mainstream schools. This encompassed the use of an assessment form, the Reintegration Readiness Scale (RRS). (This was subsequently developed into a Coping in Schools Scale covering the aspects: 'self-management of behaviour'; 'self and others'; 'self-awareness'; 'self-confidence'; 'self-organisation'; 'attitude'; 'learning skills'; and 'literacy skills'.) The RRS includes the opportunity for the pupil to assess himself. After the pupil had been assessed as being possibly ready for reintegration into mainstream school, preparation took place. This entailed setting targets developed using the RRS assessment based on remaining areas of weakness, and joining a reintegration group. This group, which met once a week, aimed, among other things, to enable each pupil to set his own targets, assess his own progress and prepare for mainstream school (p. 21). A support structure was established once the pupil had transferred to mainstream school; for example, the special school support teacher met once a week with a key person from the mainstream school to discuss the pupil's progress and to offer advice and support as necessary (p. 23). Parents were involved at all stages.

A framework involving assessment (using the Coping in Schools Scale), preparation (including group work) and support is used in various other contexts. At primary–secondary school transfer, it is employed with pupils whom the primary school identifies as at risk of not coping with the transfer to secondary school.

Where a learning support unit is provided in one school for use by several local schools, the assessment, preparation and support structure involves the pupil being assessed (using the Coping in Schools Scale) to determine whether he might benefit from support in or by the learning support unit. The structure allows reintegration into some lessons with support in the learning support unit or full reintegration with support in class.

The common assessment form is also used as part of a baseline assessment for PSPs for pupils at risk of exclusion from mainstream and also in relation to dual placements of pupils in a mainstream school and a pupil referral unit. Similarly, for pupils attending a pupil referral unit, an assessment is used (the RRS) as well as group work (a reintegration group) to help pupils prepare for reintegration into mainstream school. This is followed by post-transfer support (p. 94).

A further structure to facilitate effective provision for pupils with BESD is the model of behaviour support developed in Flintshire (Farrell, 2004, pp. 96–9). It indicates a progressive approach to supporting pupils with BESD in mainstream and the role of special schools in the structure.

The model envisages the *Special Educational Needs Code of Practice* (DfES, 2001a) level of School Action as including certain prerequisites in the mainstream school. These refer to certain policies, agreements, plans and circulars. The school is expected to have a whole-school behaviour policy; an anti-bullying policy; a drugs and alcohol policy; and a child protection policy. It should also have a formal home–school agreement. The school should have classroom management plans and IBPs. Also, it should follow the guidance of *Circular 10/99: Social Inclusion: Pupil Support* (DfEE, 1999a) concerning the law and good practice on pupil behaviour and discipline, reducing the risk of pupil disaffection, school attendance and registration, detention, the proper use of exclusion and the reintegration of excluded pupils.

If the policies, agreements, plans and the *Circular 10/99* guidance are followed, this is expected to have a positive impact on provision for pupils. Should it not, then further action is warranted. This includes developing and implementing an IBP. Should this not have the desired effect, the pupil is considered to be at School Action Plus part of the SEN graduated response.

At Action Plus various agencies are involved and information is exchanged to try to reveal the causes of the behaviour and possible solutions. Drawing on such support, internal and external to the LEA, the school implements an agreed staged model from the behaviour policy. This involves following the LEA recommendations concerning pupils who do not respond and this leads to a behaviour planning meeting to develop a PSP. (The school produces a PSP before calling in outside agencies.)

If the school-based support programme is not effective, this can lead to referral to the behaviour planning group, a local authority group. This in turn may lead to either of three alternatives:

◆ school-based education;
◆ LEA-based education support; or
◆ special education selection.

School-based education may involve the use of the school-based PSP; reintegration; education based in school with support for a specified limited time; school monitoring; and referral to the disciplinary committee.

LEA support may involve so-called 'engaged pupils' and 'non-engaged pupils'. The behaviour support service, the education welfare service and educational psychologists may provide help for engaged pupils. For non-engaged pupils, provision may involve home tuition, Youth Access or education outside the school.

With regard to special education selection, the pupil is referred for statutory assessment and may receive a statement of SEN. Support may be provided in school, or specialised support may given. The specialist support might include a combination of learning support, behaviour support and support from the educational service based on the outcome of the assessment. It could include using a PSP as well as an IEP. Alternatively, the pupil may be educated in a special school either within the LEA or in another LEA. The model may be supported by provision in pupil referral units accessed via the Behaviour Planning Group.

Justifying interventions

A general justification of interventions is likely to have two elements, one explanatory and one pragmatic. First, the intervention should look or sound as though it *ought* to work. It should be possible, indeed fairly easy, to explain it and why it works. For example, if a child finds it difficult to sustain attention, then interventions such as minimising classroom distractions and ensuring that learning tasks enable attention seem likely to be ones that should work. If explanations require leaps of faith or are propagated by charismatic discoverers of a technique who consider scrutiny damaging to the approach, practitioners and anyone else should exercise great caution. Similarly, if interventions relate to vague or unsubstantiated guesses about brain activity or are wrapped in impenetrable jargon, care is required. The book *Controversial Issues in Special Education* by Gary Hornby and his colleagues (Hornby *et al.*, 1997) forms a sobering corrective for anyone tempted by fad 'treatments' or for that matter fad 'diagnoses'.

Second, there should be evidence that the approach or intervention *has* worked. Reading about an approach and then visiting a special school, unit, mainstream school or other venue where it is being used and is working provides useful information for the teacher and others. One needs to be clear about what the expression, 'an approach is working', means. Is the intervention teaching the child skills or knowledge that is deemed necessary? Is it helping to eliminate unwanted behaviour? Is it helping the child to understand her emotions better? Is it enabling learning to take place more effectively? It is also necessary to consider the extent to which an approach that appears to be successful in one venue can be applied to another venue and with other children. Is it important that the children with whom it is proposed to introduce a new intervention are similar (in age, cognitive level for example) to those with whom the approach is working successfully?

Progress, achievement and attainment will indicate the success of interventions as they indicate the success of education for all children. Achievement is understood in broad terms to include progress in personal, emotional and social development. As approaches are used, the school will continually monitor and evaluate the effect on pupils' progress, achievement and attainment and refine and improve, or change, provision accordingly.

In summary then, one is looking for interventions that look as though they ought to work and also do work with certain pupils. One then considers whether the intervention looks as though it is likely to work with proposed pupils. This may lead one to be overcautious about approaches that look as though they ought not to work but in fact do, or approaches that do not work in one setting and with one group of pupils but may well do so in another with other pupils. But focusing on interventions that both make sense and are shown to work should help form a secure basis on which to build and refine a pedagogy across the LEA, the school and the classroom.

THINKING POINTS

Readers may wish to consider:

◆ what constitutes a credible and coherent approach to the education of pupils with BESD;
◆ the evidence that would provide a secure basis for interventions, both explanatory and pragmatic.

KEY TEXT

Hornby, G., Atkinson, M. and Howard, J. (1997) *Controversial Issues in Special Education*, London, David Fulton Publishers.

This book examines controversial approaches in special education and makes practical suggestions about how professionals and others can evaluate claims made for what are sometimes fad 'treatments'.

Addresses

The Association for Dance Movement Therapy UK
Administration
32 Meadfoot Lane
Torquay
Devon TQ1 2BQ
e-mail: queries@admt.org.uk
www.admt.org.uk

> ADMTUK involves a national network of sub-committees. Its work includes quarterly workshops, conferences and seminars; professional registration; education and training; and publications such as *e-motion* and research.

The Association of Educational Psychologists
26 The Avenue
Durham DH1 4ED

Tel: 0191 384 9512
Fax: 0191 386 5287
e-mail: aep@aep.org.uk
www.aep.org.uk

> The AEP is the professional association for educational psychologists in England and Wales and Northern Ireland.

The Association of Professional Music Therapists
61 Church Hill Road
East Barnet
Herts EN4 8SY

Tel/fax: 020 8440 4153
e-mail: APMToffice@aol.com
www.apmt.org

The APMT supports and develops the profession of music therapy. Its members are qualified music therapists who have taken a recognised post-graduate training course in music therapy. The association aims to maintain high standards of practice through administering and monitoring a range of professional development schemes.

The Association of Workers for Children with Emotional and Behavioural Difficulties
SEBDA
Church House
1 St Andrew's View
Penrith
Cumbria CA11 7YF

Tel: 01768 210 510
e-mail: admin@sebda.org
www.sebda.org

The AWCEBD is a multi-disciplinary association for teachers, residential social workers, psychologists, psychotherapists, researchers and others working with children and young people having BESD. It offers training and advice on policy development to members and publishes a journal, *Therapeutic Care and Education*.

Attention Deficit Disorder Information and Support Service
PO Box 340
Edgware
Middlesex HA8 9HL

Tel: 020 8905 2013
Fax: 020 8386 6466
e-mail: info@addiss.co.uk
www.addiss.co.uk

The service provides information and support to parents, teachers and others and information concerning books, videos and support groups.

British Association for Counselling and Psychotherapy
1 Regent Place
Rugby
Warwickshire CV21 2PJ

Tel: 0870 443 5252
Fax: 0870 443 5160
Minicom: 0870 443 5162
e-mail: bacp@bacp.co.uk
www.bacp.co.uk

The Association promotes counselling and the maintenance of standards of training and practice. It provides information on training and maintains lists of counsellors in different local areas which can be obtained by sending the Association a stamped self-addressed envelope or logging on to the website. A specialist division, Counselling in Education, provides support for practitioners in schools or the youth services.

The British Association of Art Therapists
The Claremont Project
24–7 White Lion Street
London N1H 9PD

Tel: 020 7686 4216
Fax: 020 7837 7945
e-mail: info@baat.org
www.baat.co.uk

The BAAT provides information to its members and to the public concerning all aspects of art therapy. It publishes a journal, *Inscape*, and oversees standards of training and professional practice.

The British Association of Drama Therapists
41 Broomhouse Lane
London SW6 3DP

Tel/fax: 020 7731 0160
e-mail: info@badth.org.uk
www.badth.org.uk

The British Association of Play Therapists
31 Cedar Drive
Keynsham
Bristol BS31 2TY
Tel/fax: 01179 860 390
e-mail: info@bapt.uk.com
www.bapt.info

The Association provides a support network for play therapists and information on training courses.

The British Association of Psychotherapists
37 Mapesbury Road
London NW2 4JH

Tel: 020 8452 9823
Fax: 020 8452 5182

e-mail: mail@bap-psychotherapy.org
www.bap-psychotherapy.org

The British Psychoanalytic Society
112a Shirland Road
London W9 2EQ

Tel: 020 7563 5000
Fax: 020 7563 5001
e-mail: editors@psychoanalysis.org.uk
www.psychoanalysis.org.uk

British Psychological Society
St Andrew's House
48 Princess Road East
Leicester LE1 7DR

Tel: 0116 254 9568
Fax: 0116 247 0787
e-mail: bps1@le.ac.uk
www.bps.org.uk

> The BPS is the professional body for psychologists in the United Kingdom, having various sub-groups and divisions. It publishes monthly the magazine *Psychologist*, which is of generic interest to psychologists. Its specialist journals include *The British Journal of Clinical Psychology* and *The British Journal of Educational Psychology*.

The British Society for Music Therapy
61 Church Hill Road
East Barnet
Herts EN4 8SY

Tel: 020 8441 6226
Fax: 020 8441 4118
e-mail: info@bsmt.org
www.bsmt.org

> The BSMT organises courses, conferences, workshops and meetings concerning music therapy, which are open to all. An information booklet giving details of music therapy, training courses, books and meetings is available to enquirers. The BSMT has its own publications and offers music therapy books for sale. Members receive *The British Journal of Music Therapy* and the *BSMT Bulletin*.

Essex County Council Learning Service
PO Box 47
County Hall
Chelmsford CM2 6WN

Harcourt Assessment (The Psychological Corporation)
Halley Court
Jordan Hill
Oxford OX2 8EJ

Tel: 01865 888 188
Fax: 01865 314 348
e-mail: info@harcourt-uk.com
www.harcourt-uk.com

> Harcourt Assessment are test suppliers whose assessments include ones relevant to behaviour and to ADHD.

The National Pyramid Trust for Children
84 Uxbridge Road
London W13 8RA

Tel/fax: 020 8579 5108
e-mail: enquiries@nptrust.org.uk
www.nptrust.org.uk

> The Trust aims to help primary school-aged children to fulfil their potential by building their skills, confidence and self-esteem. Their approach is based on a needs assessment, multi-disciplinary meetings and therapeutic group work (the pyramid club).

NFER-Nelson
The Chiswick Centre
414 Chiswick High Road
London W4 5TF

Tel: 020 8996 8444
Fax: 020 8996 5358
e-mail: edu&hsc@nfer-Nelson.co.uk
www.nfer-nelson.co.uk

> NFER-Nelson are test suppliers whose tests include ones relevant to BESD.

Partnership for Children
26–7 Market Place
Kingston-upon-Thames
Surrey KT1 1JH

Tel: 020 8974 6004
Fax: 020 8974 6600
e-mail: info@partnershipforchildren.org.uk
www.partnershipforchildren.org.uk

> Produces *Zippy's Friends* a programme aiming to teach coping skills to children aged 6 and 7.

The Royal College of Psychiatrists
17 Belgrave Square
London SW1X 8PG

Tel: 020 7235 2351
Fax: 020 7245 1231
e-mail: rcpsych@rcpsych.ac.uk
www.rcpsych.ac.uk

The Secure Accommodation Network
c/o Sutton Place Safe Centre
347 Salthouse Road
Hull HU8 9HR

Tel: 01482 374 186
Fax: 01482 712 173
e-mail: roy.walker@hullcc.gov.uk

> The SANE has no offices of its own but the chairperson's role rotates between secure unit managers who use their unit address. The address above is therefore that of the incumbent at the time of publication.

Tourette Syndrome (UK) Association
PO Box 26149
Dunfirmline KY12 7YU

Helpline: 0845 458 1252
Admin: 01383 629 600
e-mail: enquiries@tsa.org.uk
www.tsa.org.uk

> The association provides a helpline, membership forums, family networking, publications and advice.

Bibliography

Ali, D. *et al.* (1997) *Behaviour in Schools: A Framework for Intervention*, Birmingham, Birmingham Education Department.

American Psychiatric Association (2000) *Diagnostic and Statistical Manual of Mental Disorders – Text Revision (DSM-IV-TR)* (4th edn), Washington DC, APA.

Antidote (2003) *The Emotional Literacy Handbook*, London, David Fulton Publishers.

Ayers, H. and Prytys, C. (2002) *An A to Z Practical Guide to Emotional and Behavioural Difficulties*, London, David Fulton Publishers.

Bandura, A. (1969) *Principles of Behaviour Modification*, New York, Holt, Rinehart and Winston.

—— (1977) *Social Learning Theory*, Englewood Cliffs, NJ, Prentice-Hall.

Barkley, R. (1997) *ADHD and the Nature of Self Control*, New York, Guilford.

Bateman, A. and Holmes, J. (1995) *Introduction to Psychoanalysis: Contemporary Theory and Practice*, London, Routledge.

Beck, A. T., Rich, A. J., Shaw, B. F. and Emery, G. (1979) *Cognitive Theory of Depression*, New York, Wiley.

Blum, P. (2001) *A Teacher's Guide to Anger Management*, London, RoutledgeFalmer.

Booth, T. and Ainscow, M. with Black-Hawkins, K. (2000) *Index for Inclusion*, Bristol, Centre for Inclusive Education.

Borger, N. and Van der Meer, J. (2000) 'Visual behaviour of ADHD children during an attention test', *Journal of Child Psychology and Psychiatry*, 41(4): 525–32.

Bowlby, J. (1965) *Child Care and the Growth of Love* (2nd edn), Harmondsworth, Penguin Books.

—— (1969) *Attachment and Loss Volume 1: Attachment*, London, Hogarth Press.

—— (1973) *Attachment and Loss Volume 2: Separation, Anxiety and Anger*, London, Hogarth Press.

—— (1980) *Attachment and Loss Volume 3: Loss, Sadness and Depression*, London, Hogarth Press.

Boxall, M. (2002) *Nurture Groups in School: Principles and Practice*, London, Paul Chapman Publishing.

British Psychological Society (2000) *AD/HD: Guidelines and Principles for Successful Multi-Agency Working*, Leicester, BPS.

Bunt, L. and Hoskyns, S. (eds) (2002) *The Handbook of Music Therapy*, London, Routledge

Carrol, A. and Robertson, M. (2000) *Tourette Syndrome: A Practical Guide for Teachers, Parents and Carers*, London, David Fulton Publishers.

Cartright, N. (1996) 'Combating bullying in school: the role of peer helpers', in Cowrie, H. and Sharpe, S. (eds) *Peer Counselling in Schools*, London, David Fulton Publishers.

Case, C. and Daley, T. (1992) *The Handbook of Art Therapy*, London, Routledge.

Connors, C. K. (1996) *Connors' Rating Scales Revised*, Oxford, The Psychological Corporation.

Cooper, P. and O'Regan, F. J. (2001) *Educating Children with AD/HD*, London, RoutledgeFalmer.

Dallo, R. and Draper, R. (2000) *An Introduction to Family Therapy*, Oxford, Oxford University Press.

Daniels, A. and Williams, H. (2000) 'Reducing the need for exclusions and statements for behaviour: the Framework for Intervention Part 1', *Educational Psychology in Practice*, 15(4) (January 2000).

Department for Education and Employment (1999a) *Circular 10/99: Social Inclusion: Pupil Support*, London, DfEE.

—— (1999b) *Circular 11/99: Social Inclusion: The LEA Role in Pupil Support*, London, DfEE.

Department for Education and Skills (2001a) *Special Educational Needs Code of Practice*, London, DfES.

—— (2001b) *Inclusive Schooling: Children with Special Educational Needs*, London, DfES.

—— (2003) *Data Collection by Type of Special Educational Needs*, London, DfES.

—— (2004) *National Statistics First Release: Special Educational Needs in England, January 2004 (SFR44/2004)*, DfES. Available at www.dfes.gov.uk/rsgateway/DB/SFR/ (accessed 11 July 2005).

Dobson, K. S. and Dozois, D. J. A. (2003) 'Historical and philosophical bases of cognitive-behavioural therapies', in Dobson, K. S. (ed.) *Handbook of Cognitive-Behavioural Therapies* (2nd edn), London, Guilford Press

Dowling, E. and Osborne, E. (eds) (1994) *The Family and the School: A Joint Systems Approach to Problems with Children* (2nd edn), London, Routledge.

D'Zurilla, T. J. (1986) *Problem Solving Therapy*, New York, Springer Publishing.

Edwards, D. (2004) *Art Therapy*, London, Sage Publications.

Ellis, A., Gordon, J., Neenan, M. and Palmer, S. (1997) *Stress Counselling: A Rational Emotive Behaviour Approach*, London, Cassell.

Essex Local Education Authority (1999) *Circle of Friends* (video and literature), Chelmsford, Essex LEA.

Farrell, M. (2000) 'Educational inclusion and raising standards', *British Journal of Special Education*, 27(1) (March 2000): 35–8.

—— (2003) *The Special Education Handbook* (3rd edn), London, David Fulton Publishers.

—— (2004) *Inclusion at the Crossroads: Special Education Concepts and Values*, London, David Fulton Publishers.

——, Kerry, T. and Kerry C. (1995) *The Blackwell Handbook of Education*, Oxford, Blackwell Publishers.

Fox, G. (2001) *Supporting Children with Behaviour Difficulties: A Guide for Assistants in Schools*, London, David Fulton Publishers.

Frederickson, N. and Cline, T. (2002) *Special Educational Needs: Inclusion and Diversity: A Textbook*, Buckingham, Open University Press.

Freud, S. (2003 [1940]) *An Outline of Psychoanalysis* (translation Ragg-Kirby, H.), London, Penguin Books.

Freud, S. and Breuer, J. (1987 [1893–5]) *Studies on Hysteria*, London, Penguin Freud Library III.

Gartner, A. and Lipsky, D. K. (1989) 'New conceptualisations for special education', *European Journal of Special Needs Education*, 4(1): 16–21.

Geldard, K. and Geldard, D. (1997) *Counselling Children*, London, Sage.

—— and —— (2001) *Working with Children in Groups*, Basingstoke, Palgrave.

Goodman, R. (1997) 'The strengths and difficulties questionnaire: a research note', *Journal of Child Psychology and Psychiatry*, 38: 581–5.

—— (1999) 'The extended version of the strengths and difficulties questionnaire as a guide to child psychiatric caseness and consequent burden', *Journal of Child Psychology and Psychiatry*, 40(5): 791–800.

Gordan, T. (1974) *TET: Teacher Effectiveness Training*, New York, David McKay.

Greenhill, L. (1998) 'Childhood ADHD: pharmacological treatments', in Nathan, P. and Gorman, M. (eds) *A Guide to Treatments that Work*, Oxford, Oxford University Press.

Greenwood, C. (2002) *Understanding the Needs of Parents: Guidelines for Effective Collaboration with Parents of Children with Special Educational Needs*, London, David Fulton Publishers.

Gurman, A. S. and Messer, S. B. (eds) (2003) *Essential Psychotherapies: Theory and Practice*, London, Guilford Press.

Hampshire County Council (1996) Private communication.

Hargie, O., Saunders, C. and Dickson, D. (1994) *Social Skills in Interpersonal Communication* (3rd edn), London, Routledge.

Hayes, S. C., Follette, W. C. and Follette, V. M. (1995) 'Behaviour therapy: a conceptual approach' in Gurman, A. S. and Messer, S. B. (eds) *Essential Psychotherapies: Theory and Practice* (1st edn), London, Guilford Press

Hill, P. and Cameron, M. (1999) 'Recognising hyperactivity: a guide for the cautious clinician', *Child Psychology and Psychiatry Review*, 4(2): 50–60.

Holmes, J. (1993) *John Bowlby and Attachment Theory*, London, Routledge.

Hornby, G. (2003) 'Counselling and guidance of parents', in G. Hornby, C. Hall and E. Hall (2 edn) *Counselling Pupils in Schools: Skills and Strategies for Teachers*, London. RoutledgeFalmer, pp. 129–40.

——, Atkinson, M. and Howard, J. (1997) *Controversial Issues in Special Education*, London, David Fulton Publishers.

——, Hall, C. and Hall, E. (2003) *Counselling Pupils in Schools: Skills and Strategies for Teachers*, London, RoutledgeFalmer.

Irlen, H. L. (1994) 'Scotopic sensitivity/Irlen syndrome hypothesis and explanation of the syndrome', *Journal of Behavioural Optometry*, 5: 65–6.

Kelly, B. (1999) 'Circle Time – a systems approach to emotional and behavioural difficulties', *Educational Psychology in Practice*, 15(1): 40–4.

Lawrence, D. (1996) *Enhancing Self-esteem in the Classroom* (2nd edn), London, David Fulton Publishers.

Lewis, A. (2004) 'And when did you last see your father? Exploring the views of children with learning difficulties/disabilities', *British Journal of Special Education*, 31(1): 3–9.

McFarlane, P. (2005) *Drama Therapy: Raising Children's Self Esteem and Developing Emotional Stability*, London, David Fulton Publishers.

McLaughlin, C., Clarke, P. and Chisholm, M. (1996) *Counselling and Guidance in Schools: Developing Policy and Practice*, London, David Fulton Publishers.

McNamara, S. and Moreton, G. (2001) *Changing Behaviour: Teaching Children with Emotional and Behaviour Difficulties in Primary and Secondary Classrooms* (2nd edn), London, David Fulton Publishers.

McSherry, J. (2001) *Challenging Behaviours in Mainstream Schools: Practical Strategies for Effective Intervention and Reintegration*, London, David Fulton Publishers.

Maines, B. and Robinson, G. (1998) *B/G Steem: A Self Esteem Scale with Locus of Control Items*, London, Lucky Duck Publishing.

Mischel, W. (1968) *Personality and Assessment*, New York, Wiley.

Morris, E. (2002) *Insight Secondary: Assessing and Developing Self-esteem in Young People Aged 11–16*, Windsor, NFER-Nelson.

Mosley, J. (1996) *Quality Circle Time in the Primary Classroom*, Cambridge, LDA.

—— and Tew, M. (1999) *Quality Circle Time in the Secondary School: A Handbook of Good Practice*, London, David Fulton Publishers.

Munden, A. and Arcelus, J. (1999) *The AD/HD Handbook*, London, Jessica Kingsley.

National Institute of Clinical Excellence (2000) *Guidance on the Use of Methylphenidate for AD/HD*, London, NICE.

Nelson-Jones, R. (2005) *Introduction to Counselling Skills and Activities* (2nd edn), London, Sage.

Newton, C. and Wilson, D. (1999) *Circle of Friends*, London, Folens.

Nigg, J. and Hinshaw, S. (1998) 'Parent personality traits and psychopathology associated with anti-social behaviours in childhood ADHD', *Journal of Child Psychology and Psychiatry*, 39(2): 145–59.

Pellegrini, A. and Horvat, M. (1995) 'A developmental and contextualist critique of AD/HD', *Educational Researcher*, 249(10): 13–20.

——, Huberty, P. and Jones, I. (1996) 'The effects of recess timing on children's playground and classroom behaviours', *American Educational Research Journal*, 32(4): 845–64.

Place, M., Wilson, J., Martin, E. and Hulsmeir, J. (2000) 'The frequency of emotional and behavioural disturbance in an EBD school', *Child Psychology and Psychiatry Review*, 5(2): 76–80.

Seifert, J., Scheuerpflug, P., Zillerssen, K. E., Fallgater, A. and Warnke, A. (2003) 'Electrophysiological investigations of the effectiveness of methylphenidate in children with and without ADHD', *Journal of Neural Transmission*, 110(7): 821–8.

Skinner, B. F. (1968) *The Technology of Teaching*, New York, Appleton-Century-Crofts.

—— (1974) *About Behaviourism*, London, Jonathan Cape.

Spiegler, M. D. and Guivrement, D. C. (1998) *Contemporary Behaviour Therapy* (3rd edn), Pacific Grove, CA, Brooks/Cole.

Tannock, R. (1998) 'ADHD: advances in cognitive, neurobiological and genetic research', *Journal of Child Psychology and Psychiatry*, 39(1): 65–99.

Taylor, G. (1997) 'Community building in schools: developing a circle of friends', *Educational and Child Psychology*, 14: 45–50.

Tilstone, C. and Layton, L. (2004) *Child Development and Teaching Pupils with Special Educational Needs*, London, Routledge.

Wade, J. (1999) 'Including all learners: QCA's approach', *British Journal of Special Education*, 26(2): 80–2.

Wallace, B. and Crawford, S. (1994) 'Instructional paradigms and the ADHD child', in Weaver, C. (ed.) *Success at Last: Helping Students with AD(H)D Achieve Their Potential*, Portsmouth, NH, Heinemann.

World Health Organization (1990) *International Classification of Diseases* (10th edn), Geneva, WHO.

Index

ABC (activating event, beliefs,
  consequences) analysis 36, 39
ABC (antecedent, behaviour,
  consequences) approach 50
'actor observer effect' 38
ADHD *see* attention deficit hyperactivity
  disorder
age-related interventions 74
Ali, D. 22–3
allergies, ADHD 70
American Psychiatric Association (APA)
  63–4
anger management training 38–9
Antidote 31–2
anxiety management 30, 34–5, 46, 74
anxious-avoidance/ambivalence 57
APA *see* American Psychiatric Association
art therapy 55–6, 60
assessment 21, 30, 42–3, 54; ADHD 64–5;
  SEN 4
Association of Play Therapists 54–5
attachment theory 56–7
attention deficit hyperactivity disorder
  (ADHD) 63–6; interventions 66–71
attributions, negative/positive 34, 35, 38
audit, behavioural 22–3
avoidance conditioning 44
Ayers, H. 23

Bandura, A. 46–7
BDPs *see* behaviour development plans
Beck, Aaron 36–7
behavioural approach 35–6, 41–3, 73, 74;
  ADHD 66–7; interventions 43–50
behavioural audit 22–3

behaviour, challenging 6–7, 50, 75–6
behaviour development plans (BDPs) 22
behaviour environment plans (BEPs) 22–3
Behaviour in Schools framework 22–3
belief systems 20
BEPs *see* behaviour environment plans
B/G Steem checklist 33
biofeedback, ADHD 68
Bowlby, John 56, 57
brain dysfunction, ADHD 65–6, 69–70
Breuer, Joseph 60

catharsis 60–1
causal attributions 38
causal factors: 8–9, 20, 42, 54; ADHD
  65–6
challenging behaviour 6–7, 50, 75–6
Children's Trusts 13–14
Circle of Friends 25–6, 35
circle of interaction 18
circle time 25
circular causality 18
circular questioning 21
Circulars 10/99, 11/9: Social Inclusion 10–
  11, 77
classroom environment, ADHD 67–8
cognitive appraisal 38–9
cognitive approach 29–30, 73, 74;
  interventions 31–9
cognitive-behavioural perspective 35–6
cognitive development 74
cognitive schemas 37
cognitive therapy 36–7
communication 58–9, 60, 68
compensatory skills 69

Connors' Rating Scales (Revised) 65
contracts 47–8
Coping in Schools programme 24,
    75–6
counselling 34, 57–60
curriculum 60–1
cycle of interaction 18

Daniels, A. 22
*Data Collection by Type of Special
    Educational Needs* 4–5, 8
Department for Education and
    Employment (DfEE) 10–11, 77
Department for Education and Skills
    (DfES) 3–5, 12, 15
desensitisation 46
*Diagnostic and Statistical Manual of the
    American Psychiatric Association
    (DSM-IV-TR)* 63–4
diet, ADHD 70
Dowling, E. 19, 20
drama therapy 56
drugs, ADHD 69–70
DSM-IV-TR 63–4

Early Support Pilot Programme (ESPP) 13
Early Years Action (Plus) 3
'ecosystemic perspective' 17
Education Act (1996) 5–6, 12–13
Ellis, Albert 36
emotional intelligence/literacy 31–3
empowering 58
engaged pupils 77
ESPP *see* Early Support Pilot Programme
event sampling 43
exclusion 11
executive functions 66
exploration 58
extinction 44

fading 45–6
'false consensus effect' 38
family links, ADHD 66
family systems 9, 14–15, 19–20, 26–7, 73,
    74
family therapy 17–18, 26
feedback, ADHD 68
Feingold diet 70
food allergies, ADHD 70
Fox, Glenys 37
frameworks for intervention 22–3, 75–6
Freud, Sigmund 33, 53, 60–1

generalisation 45
*Goodman Strengths and Difficulties
    Questionnaire (SDQ)* 64
group work 23–6, 35, 56–7

Hampshire LEA strategies, ADHD
    70–1
Hornby, Gary 14–15, 58, 78
'hostile attribution bias' 38
hyperactivity *see* attention deficit
    hyperactivity disorder
hypnosis 60–1

IBPs *see* individual behaviour plans
identification 20–1, 30, 42–3, 54;
    ADHD 64–5
identity 33
IEPs *see* individual education plans
imitation 46
impulsivity *see* attention deficit
    hyperactivity disorder
inclusion 10–13
Inclusive Schooling 12
individual behaviour plans (IBPs) 23
individual education plans (IEPs) 11, 15,
    23
intervention frameworks 22–3,
    75–6
intervention overviews 7–8, 73–8

Kelly, B. 25

language, emotions 31, 32–3
learning approaches, ADHD 68–9
LEAs *see* local education authorities
Lesch-Nyhan syndrome 7
Lewis, A. 15
listening skills 59
literacy, emotional 31–3
local education authorities (LEAs) 4, 11,
    74, 77

McNamara, S. 19
McSherry, J. 24, 75–6
mainstream schools 10–13, 76–7
medication, ADHD 69–70
Mischel, W. 47
modelling 46–7
Moreno, Jacob 21
Moreton, G. 19
movement therapy 56
music therapy 55

National Children's Trust Framework 13
negative attributions 34, 35, 38
negative perceptions 30
negative reinforcement 44
non-engaged pupils 77
nurture groups 56–7

observational learning 47
Osborne, E. 19, 20
over-correction 44, 45

paraphrasing 59
parental collaboration 14–15
Partnership for Children 32
pastoral support programmes (PSPs) 11, 77
peer counselling 59–60
phobias 46
PLASC *see* Pupil Level Annual School
    Census
play therapy 54–5
positive reinforcement 44
prevalence: 9–10; ADHD 65
problem-solving approaches 37
professional co-operation 13–14
Prytys, C. 23
PSPs *see* pastoral support programmes
psychodynamic approach 53–4, 73, 74;
    interventions 54–61
punishment 44, 48
Pupil Level Annual School Census
    (PLASC) (DfES) 4–5, 8
pupil participation 15

rational-emotive behavioural therapy
    (REBT) 36
reattributions 34, 35, 38
REBT *see* rational-emotive behavioural
    therapy
reflective listening 59
reinforcement 43–5
reintegration groups 24
Reintegration Readiness Scale (RRS) 76
repression 61
'response cost' 48
rewards 44, 48
Ritalin, ADHD 69–70
RRS *see* Reintegration Readiness Scale
rules, school and family 19–20

schedules of reinforcement 45
schemas, cognitive 37
School Action (Plus) 3–4, 10, 58,
    77
school–family liaison workers
    26–7
school phobia 46
schools: inclusion 10–13; emotionally
    literate 31–2; support 76–7
school systems 18–20, 26–7
*SDQ see Goodman Strengths and
    Difficulties Questionnaire*
self-attributions 34, 35, 38
self-concept 30
self-efficacy 47
self-esteem 25, 33–4
self-regulation 47, 66
self-talk 34–5
SEN *see* special educational needs
social inclusion 10–11
social learning theory 46–7
social skills training 48–50, 69
sociometric assessment 21
special educational needs (SEN) 3–5;
    legal definition 5–6
Special Educational Needs and Disability
    Act (2001) 12
*Special Educational Needs Code of
    Practice* 3–4, 7, 15, 76
specialist counselling 58
specialist intervention 13–14, 26
stimulant drugs, ADHD 69–70
systems approach 17–21, 73, 74;
    interventions 21–7

teaching approaches, ADHD 68–9
therapies 54; art 55–6, 60; cognitive 36–7;
    drama 56; family 17–18, 26; movement
    56; music 55; play 54–5
time out 45
time sampling 42–3
token economy 48
Tourette's syndrome 7

Williams, H. 22
Wolpe, Joseph 46

Zippy's Friends 32